Justice For William

THE STORY OF WENDY CROMPTON: MOTHER OF A MURDERED SON

Justice For William
The Story of Wendy Crompton: Mother of a Murdered Son
Helen P Simpson

Published by
WATERSIDE PRESS LTD
Sherfield Gables
Hook
Hampshire RG27 OJG
United Kingdom

Orders and enquiries

WATERSIDE PRESS
Domum Road
Winchester SO23 9NN
United Kingdom

Telephone 01962 855567 UK Landline local-cost calls 0845 2300 733
E-mail enquiries@watersidepress.co.uk
Online catalogue and bookstore www.watersidepress.co.uk

ISBN 9781904380306

Cataloguing-In-Publication Data A catalogue record for this book can be obtained from the British Library.

Cover design Waterside Press Ltd. Main photograph: Castle Hill, West Yorkshire.

Printing and binding CPI Antony Rowe, Chippenham and Eastbourne

North American distributors International Specialised Book Services (ISBS), 920 NE 58th Ave, Suite 300, Portland, Oregon, 97213-3786, USA
Telephone 1 800 944 6190 Fax 1 503 280 8832 orders@isbs.com www.isbs.com

Justice For William

THE STORY OF WENDY CROMPTON: MOTHER OF A MURDERED SON

Helen P Simpson

With a Foreword by Terry Waite CBE

WATERSIDE PRESS

Acknowledgements

Our thanks go to Tim Newell and Terry Waite for supporting our aims to have this story published.

Helen P Simpson
Wendy Crompton

November 2006

CONTENTS

About those involved: A Note

Wendy Crompton's son William and his girlfriend Fiona were killed in an horrendous attack by another young man on 2 May 1996 when William was just 18 years old. Her experience of what followed is set out in this book which tells of Wendy's long, hard fight to achieve justice for William and how, as a secondary victim of crime she was treated in ways that ranged from insensitivity to prejudice and lack of respect. She now campaigns for and helps other people who have been affected by homicide, including to challenge those aspects of the criminal justice system that fail people like her - by sitting on steering groups and committees, giving presentations and lobbying for improvements. She also carries out a good deal of other voluntary work. She has three other children, Marc (26), Christopher (24) and Wendy-Lou (23) - all of whom feature in this book.

Helen P Simpson the author of *Justice For William* is a community safety officer with Kirklees Safer Communities (a partnership between Kirklees Metropolitan Council, West Yorkshire Police Service, the National Probation Service, Victim Support and others) and is involved in the development and implementation of crime reduction strategies to lessen crime, disorder and the fear of crime. She first met Wendy Crompton, shortly after starting work with the Reducing Burglary Initiative (part of Victim Support) based at Huddersfield Police Station. They soon became firm friends and co-campaigners for better treatment of victims of homicide and serious crime. Helen has three children, Emily (30), Steve (28) and Andrew (23). Helen and Wendy share similar tastes in music, drama, art and literature - despite a sporting schism, Wendy being a fan of Huddersfield Giants Rugby League Club and Helen of Huddersfield Town Football Club (neither having yet succeeded in converting the other from rugby league to association football or vice-versa).

Terry Waite CBE is a leading British humanitarian and author. He is best known for his work as a hostage negotiator having been famously held hostage himself after travelling to Lebanon as an envoy for the Church of England to try and secure the release of four hostages including the journalist John McCarthy. After he arrived in Lebanon's capital, Beirut, in January 1987 intending to negotiate with the Islamic Jihad and agreed to meet the captors subject to his 'safe conduct', the group broke trust and took Waite hostage. Waite's survival in solitary confinement for more than four years until November 1991 has become legend. He is co-founder of YCare (a development agency linked to the YMCA movement), founder of Hostage UK (an organization aiming to give support to the families of hostages), a patron of the Romany Society, visiting fellow at Magdalen College, is involved with various charities including Emmaus for the homeless and was the Archbishop of Canterbury's Assistant for Anglican Communion Affairs during the primate-ship of Dr Robert Runcie. He has written three books, including *Taken on Trust*, about his years of incarceration in the Lebanon.

Foreword Terry Waite CBE

For many years now I have attempted to find an alternative to the word 'victim'. 'Injured party'; 'wounded'; 'casualty'; 'sufferer'; 'survivor', all describe a part of the experience but as yet I have not been able to find a suitable English word to adequately describe the experience of being a victim. At a recent conference in Holland I raised the issue and was told that the Dutch also struggle with this question. The Dutch word actually means 'sacrificial victim' and thus is even stronger than the English.

Not everyone who falls prey to profound misfortune wishes to be described as a victim and those who undergo the experience react in a variety of ways. Some time ago I sat with a mother whose son had been taken prisoner and beheaded. She said that that few people could understand how she, as a mother, felt at that time but, remarkably, she went on to say that her grief was no different than that of a mother who had lost her children as a result of the warfare that had led to her son's death. That compassionate old lady was able to quickly link her dreadful experience of grief and loss with that of others far away. As she did so her agony was turned into compassion and she was well on the way to being healed.

Not everyone can move so quickly and some cannot move at all. I have known other mothers who have lost a child sink into deep despair and self pity. The understandable anger they experienced has turned into bitterness and their lives have been virtually totally destroyed in the process.

Without question we live in a world where there is considerable suffering and suffering is no respecter of persons. Certainly from the time of Job onwards men and women have wrestled with the question as to why the innocent should suffer and there is nothing that I know of that answers that question completely. We are obliged to accept the fact that suffering is part and parcel of life as we know it and as human beings we all have an obligation to attempt to alleviate it. However we cannot eliminate it completely. What we can say with some confidence is that in many cases, if not in most, suffering need not destroy totally. As so many men and women have demonstrated across the ages it is possible to turn suffering around and allow it to be the ground from which a new creativity emerges. Suffering will always be difficult to experience and men and women pass through it in different ways and at their own pace. The range of emotions experienced by the victims of suffering varies in degree. Some experience anger that virtually blinds them or at best distorts their perceptions regarding the behaviour and motives of others. Some feel totally empty and simply wish for death.

The immediate victim is of course not the only one affected by suffering. The professional police officer, prison officer, lawyer, Victim Support worker - all of whom face suffering on a daily basis - have to find their own way of coping with the burden. I recollect a good friend of mine who in his professional life had to deal with an unusual number of criminal sex cases telling me that he needed support to cope with the burden that was put on him each week. He had enough insight to get help when he needed it. There are others who cope by putting up a shield between themselves and the victim and thus may appear brusque and uncaring. Some of the elaborate procedures enacted in the courtrooms of our land have developed partly to protect those who work there on a daily basis. Of course the procedures need to be kept constantly under review, just as any counsellor will need to be aided and supported to reflect not only on his or her own behaviour in relation to other people but also the effect that this work is having on them personally and on various aspects of their own lives.

Helen P Simpson's account of 'The Story of Wendy Crompton' graphically illustrates the points I have made above and many more besides. It is frank, at times horrifying and pulls no punches. Some may think some of the comments made about certain individuals who feature in the story to be somewhat harsh or the recorded behaviour of some officials seemingly casual or uncaring. In reading the book one needs to keep clearly in mind that Wendy in particular is speaking out of her own experience and that this is how she perceived events at the time. Similarly with Helen's comments as she delves deeper into how those events affected Wendy and her family. The issue is not whether the perception was 'right' or 'wrong' The point is that this was their perception at the time and this gives their comments validity.

I confess that I did not find the book comfortable reading and almost put it to one side after the first couple of chapters. I'm glad that I continued with it as it taught me to be even more understanding in relating to those who suffer. Both Wendy and Helen have made a valuable contribution to my understanding of the problems faced by the victims of crime and those who work with them. They are living proof of what I said earlier. Suffering need not destroy. Their book is a testimony to that fact.

Dedication

To William, with love.

CHAPTER 1

Tea and Coincidence

I don't think I believe in fate. Fate is some big controlling force that orders everything, whereas my view of the world as a chaotic, humdrum sort of place doesn't really allow for fate to be ordering anything. I just remember the coincidence that confronted me that day as being so big that I was spooked. It was a whopper and I felt, for a moment, like a pawn in someone else's game, as if I was being controlled. That describes my very first meeting with Wendy and it's the reason why my friendship with her has always been unique to me. My other friendships are based only on the fact that I'm very fond of these people and want them in my life. I like Wendy too and enjoy her company just as much, but there has always been this nagging doubt that I didn't choose this friendship and that neither did she. I can't quite shake off this feeling: that I was meant to be her friend and that one day I would find out why.

•   •   •

Wendy and I first met through work. Not as colleagues, that would have been a far more relaxed and normal way to meet. We met because she was another box for me to tick, another interview to get out of the way, another set of data to feed into my report. That was what I had expected that day. That was how it was supposed to be. I expected to collect the data and take it back to add to my collection. I might see her again in town one day and wonder where I'd seen her before but not be able to remember.

If anybody had told me that this was to be an unforgettable meeting that would bring about great changes in my life, I would simply not have believed them. I think Wendy might have believed it, though. She has a way of sniffing the air and saying 'I've got a feeling about this. This is going to be very important. Trust me. I'm usually right about these things.' More often than not, she is. She listens to her instincts and trusts them. My instincts are far too embarrassed about themselves to do more than whisper inaudibly into the darkness when I'm asleep so I have to make do with reflection upon the known facts of whatever matter it is. The fact of this matter is that she is right about things more often than I am.

It was her instincts that told her to agree to see me. She didn't know why. She just knew that I should go, that it was important I turned up at her house, unprepared for my life to be changed by somebody who was supposed to fill in a questionnaire and make me a cup of tea while she was at it. She might have warned me that I'd become deeply embroiled in a cause that would change my view of the world and imprison me at my desk, determined to find the most powerful ways of expressing her passions with my words. She might have warned me that she was to lead me down the path she had trodden so that I could taste the harrowing events that have shaped her life and seek the words that would influence changes to the very system that paid my wages.

I was very fond of being paid. It pleased me to be independent of the state. I was a late-comer into the employment market. I had left paid employment in my early twenties and brought up my family within the financial constraints of marriage to a partner who prioritised his own needs, liked to rule the roost and failed to grasp the whole concept of earning money and paying bills. I met him in Bristol, where I'd moved to from Huddersfield when I was eighteen years old. Moving there had seemed like a good idea at the time and that is good enough a reason for moving home when you are an eighteen-year-old.

I stayed there for sixteen years. During that time I met people who are still my closest friends today. Mal was one of the first people I got to know after I arrived in Bristol. We gossiped away from the moment we met and still carry on the conversation today, over thirty years later. We were both northerners in a southern city. You could drown a small village in the amount of tea we've got through together over the years. We shared a flat, met our partners and produced our families. Her marriage was no better or more financially secure than mine was. We may never have managed our situations at all if we hadn't had a network of friends to rely on. We borrowed things from each other, babysat for each other and supported each other through it all.

Another close friend is Jo. I met her when I was expecting my third and final child. She was on the same baby equipment-sharing circuit as me. My friend Liz brought round a crib, carry cot and huge maternity clothes for me to borrow. She instructed me not to return them because another friend of hers was four months behind me with her pregnancy and I should pass them on to her. I never used brand new equipment for my babies because I didn't have enough money. I didn't see this as a problem, though. Within our private support network we could manage by passing around all the necessary items, keeping each other's small children occupied and making each other laugh. I liked Jo as soon as I met her. She had two small children, a lazy partner, little money, a dry sense of humour and a determination to survive. She fitted perfectly into my inner circle of trusted friends and there she remains to this day.

Five years later, Jo moved to Wales and came back to visit with pictures of the area where she lived. It looked beautiful, green and small and safe. I was a country girl and hadn't really taken to bringing up children in a big city. My eldest was almost ready to start secondary school and I dreaded the thought of her struggling to settle in at a tough, inner city school. I put forward the idea of us moving to the Welsh countryside where property was cheaper and was delighted when we packed up and moved to a place forty miles from Jo. It was great to watch the children adjusting to country life. Looking back, I'm sure they would have been fine in the city but it was good to let them loose for a while in a place where it didn't matter what label was on your trainers but important that your wellies didn't leak.

I settled down easily enough and soon had a close circle of friends with whom I enjoyed spending time but there were clouds on the horizon. Not little fluffy grey rain clouds. This was a gathering storm. I could feel my marriage coming to the end of its natural life. I had spent years organising my life in such a way as to be happy within an unsuccessful marriage, but what had become a sour relationship began to infect my days and could no longer be ignored. The profit from the sale of the house in Bristol had dwindled away, my husband spent less time in work and more time at the pub. The growing mountain of debts cast a doom-like shadow over the household. I'd had enough. I wanted to make a secure home, where I took charge of the income and paid the bills. I wanted to be away from his bad temper and mean ways. I wanted to go home.

I had always been homesick for Huddersfield but now I desperately wanted to go back. Seven years after moving to Wales, I did just that.

•   •   •

Making such a dramatic change in my life was frightening, especially with three children and a cat to look after. I rented a house that was damp and dingy, but I wasn't too worried about that. It was home. I claimed benefits and was amazed to find myself better off financially than I had been for as long as I could remember. It wasn't much, but it was so much more than I had previously had access to. My rent and rates were paid for me by the benefits office and I had cash to use for fuel, electricity and food. I felt pathetically grateful. As a measure of poverty, the benefits system is not the least that people in our society have to live on. I knew plenty of women who were poorer than that.

The divorce was vicious. I was surprised that he made such a fuss. I had thought that the ending of the relationship might have been as much a relief for him as it was for me. After all, we didn't even like each other. I needed the help of a solicitor and was lucky to find a good one. There were many visits to the county court. I was granted injunctions (three of them, one after the other) to keep my ex away, there were child welfare reports and all manner of interventions. Legal aid paid for my solicitor's bills, which I imagined were huge. Again, I was grateful to get this help. The circumstances were awful but I discovered I liked the court. I liked the way only one person spoke at once. I liked the way everyone was polite and everything happened in a safe environment. I looked at all these people with professions and knew that I wanted to be in that situation one day.

There I was, a single parent, living in a damp rented house with very few qualifications to my name and no work experience since the mid-1970s, when people in offices had ashtrays on their desks. By now it is all no smoking, computer skills and work experience. The last time I had filled out a job application form, it asked for your name and address, qualifications and what your hobbies were. It was never going to be that easy again. I looked at my situation and realised that I had to take a huge leap if I was to get off benefits and make a living. It was the direction in which I wanted to go. I felt that society had given me a helping hand and I was glad of it. My next ambition was to be independent of the state.

From the time of my arrival back in Huddersfield, it took me another seven years to get there. After a shaky start, sorting out housing problems and generally resettling, I went to university on a part-time basis as a mature student. Between lectures and seminars I did some voluntary work for the Probation Service (now called the National Probation Service). As soon as I graduated, I was able to start work as a probation service officer. It was only a temporary contract, but at least it was a start. I was delighted to be financially independent. Nine months later I landed another temporary contract for a really interesting job with the rather impressive title 'Information Analyst'. It was part of the Reducing Burglary Initiative and my role was to interview convicted burglars and victims of burglary. I was able to design the questionnaires myself and organize my working day. I was so happy to be in work and it opened up a whole new world to me. I was determined to produce a really valuable report at the end of the year. I was based in the Victim Support office, which was in the police station. I was given details of the victims and made contact with them, explaining what I was up to and asking them if they would agree to see me.

●　　　●　　　●

One day I picked up the details of a victim of burglary. The file was marked in pen with the words 'NO CONTACT'. I asked about this and was told that Victim Support was already in touch with the victim because her son had been murdered five years ago, when she lived in Wales. She had made a complaint about the way Victim Support in Wales had done their job and it was important that she had no further cause for complaint. I felt quite insulted. I insisted that she was still a victim of burglary and that I should be able to ask her if she wanted to talk to me about it. I gave assurances that I could be sensitive and promised not to become involved in areas in which I had not received training. My argument must have been persuasive because it was agreed that I could ring the Victim Support volunteer who had been assigned to support her and put in my request to see the victim. I did this immediately and the volunteer explained that she was actually with the victim at that very moment and would speak to her straight away. She did so and then the victim spoke to me herself. Although I could sense the suspicion in her voice, she did say that I could go and talk to her. I asked if she was available that afternoon. She was.

I travelled up to her house by bus. I was having a John Cleese moment but instead of 'Don't mention the war!' I was repeating to myself, mentally, 'Don't mention the murder!' I was painfully aware that I had no training to talk to anyone who had lost someone through murder. I was putting myself in a position where I could cause all sorts of problems. I didn't want to make a mess of it. I wanted to be a real working woman, not someone who had got a job by mistake and made a complete mess of it, thus revealing myself as someone who ought to have stayed at home on benefits and not presumed to be as good as people with jobs. It was this fear, this incredulity that I had actually made the huge leap into work, which ensured that I made such an effort. I got off the bus and looked at the map. 'Don't mention the murder.' I found the house and opened the garden gate. 'Don't mention the murder' I thought as I raised my hand to knock on the door.

A young girl who looked like she was in her late teens answered my knock. She was delicate, almost frail, with that pixie look about her. She invited me in and I went into the front room. A woman who was obviously her mother looked at me in a serious, almost hostile manner but asked me if I wanted a cup of tea. She went into the kitchen and put the kettle on. I spotted an ashtray and asked if it was alright if I smoked. It was, so I rolled a cigarette. I had started rolling my own cigarettes twenty years before, when I couldn't afford to buy ready made ones. It is a habit I have been unable to change. I thought of something to say to the young girl to break the ice.

'Whereabouts in Wales do you come from?' I asked.

'Newtown,' she answered.

This was good. I knew the area. It would give us a topic of conversation.

'Oh, I've been there,' I said, 'my mate lives in Llandod' (the local name for Llandrindod Wells).

'Llandod,' repeated the girl, a look of painful disgust in her eyes. 'That's where my brother was murdered.'

I sat silently in horror, taking a deep drag on my cigarette. I'd lasted about thirty seconds before the murder was mentioned. She carried on talking as if the naming of the town had wrenched the words from her. I felt that it was my fault, I had somehow hurt her.

'It was him and his girlfriend. They were in his girlfriend's grandmother's bungalow. They were both stabbed to death.'

I immediately forgot everything else in that moment. I forgot that I wasn't going to mention the murder, I forgot that I was going to avoid getting into trouble at work, I forgot why I had come to this house. I knew this story. I'd already heard it. Well, Llandod is a small place.

'I know this,' I said, 'my mate told me about it. My friend didn't mention any names. She never broke confidentiality. She told me about it because she is my friend and she needed to talk to someone in order to off-load. There was only one person convicted of this murder, wasn't there? My friend said that the evidence suggested that two people committed it, but that this was never explained during the trial.' At this, the mother shot out of the kitchen and stared at me. I felt a moment of deep anxiety.

Her look demanded an explanation from me.

'It was Jo who told me about this case,' I explained.

'Do you know Jo?' Her face lost its frown and took on a look of amazement. 'I left Wales to get away from everything and everybody,' she said, 'I haven't let anybody know where I am. There is only one person who I regret losing touch with, though, and that is Jo.'

I felt a second or two of relief. Maybe I hadn't said the wrong thing after all.

'She was here last week,' I said. 'She came up to visit me.'

The mother was silent for a moment. Then she said, 'I got rid of my phone book. I don't have Jo's number. I thought I'd lost touch with her altogether. I've been thinking about her, though. I wished I had kept her number. I'd like to talk to her again.'

I could easily rectify this. 'I'll ring her when I get home. I'll give her your number. She can ring you.'

She stood there staring at me for a while, letting it sink in and then suddenly smiled. 'Oooh, I forgot the tea. I'll go and get you your cup of tea.' I just felt that she didn't smile very often. I'd got a smile out of her. We were going to be alright. She brought in three steaming-hot mugs of tea on a tray, one for me, one for her daughter and the last one for herself. We introduced ourselves properly this time. They were both called Wendy but little Wendy was usually called Wendy-Lou. We all had tea and cigarettes and sat for a minute or two, drinking, smoking, looking at each other and letting the amazement of this coincidence sink in, we weren't merely strangers, we were Jo's friends, we were in good company .

I realised she hadn't been making tea when she was in the kitchen. She had been standing in silence, listening to what Wendy-Lou and I were saying. We now felt the need to get to know each other. She mentioned my roll-ups, she liked the fact I wasn't 'posh'. She had expected another official to arrive in a sharp suit and with a superior attitude. She was as surprised to meet me as I was to meet her. We talked about how long I'd known Jo and whereabouts I'd lived in Wales. I was feeling more at ease, we were getting to know each other. I mentioned her accent over the second cup of tea. It wasn't Welsh. I asked where she lived before Wales. She told me she came from Warrington.

'Oh, another best mate of mine is from Warrington,' I said, 'Latchford.'

She looked shocked again. 'I'm from Latchford.'

My eyebrows went up. 'Her name is Mal Hayes. They're a big family. Do you know the Hayes?'

'I went to school with Brian,' she said, almost in a whisper.

'Ah, Brian, Mal's brother. I know Brian. He's a lovely bloke.'

We did a bit more staring at each other. I explained that Mal and Jo had heard about each other through me but they'd never actually met. This was feeling bizarre. She had connections to two of my closest friends, neither of whom had ever lived in Huddersfield or met each other. We seemed linked to each other in a web of friendship.

I was busy telling myself that this was mere coincidence but I could feel something irritating in my head, like an alarm bell ringing. A great big pointer was sitting above us with 'Notice this. This is important.' written down the side. This had not escaped Wendy.

'I wondered why I had agreed to see you,' she said, 'I wouldn't normally have agreed to let someone come round and ask questions but something told me to say "Yes". I was obviously meant to meet you.'

I wasn't used to dealing with things that are meant to happen. Fate had left me very much to my own devices and I generally believed my scepticism was a useful device that protected me from horoscopes, palm readers, religions and anybody else who marketed anything that involved lack of evidence and blind faith. I was sure that I'd be able to shrug it off as coincidence before too long but I certainly had a creepy feeling about it.

I was glad that Wendy mentioned the fact that I had gone there to ask questions, because I seemed to have forgotten my reason for being there. I got out the questionnaire, suddenly embarrassed to return to work mode. I asked one of the questions on the form: 'What items were removed?'

Wendy told me that the TV and stereo had been removed but that she didn't care about them. What she cared about was the fact that strangers had broken into her house and touched her boy's ashes. They had tried to open the container but failed. They had left the ashes behind but it outraged her that they had touched them. They had no right. Wendy had been listening to the music she was going to play at his funeral before she went away for the weekend. She had left it in the stereo so the precious CD had gone as well. The song she wanted to play was 'Where Are You Now?' by Britney Spears.

I was confused. If she had his ashes in her possession, he must already have had a funeral, but she was talking about the arrangements for a funeral that was still to come. My confusion must have been obvious. I didn't need to ask, she simply volunteered the explanation. She was quite tearless as she told me, in her flat, monotone voice that his organs had been retained without her knowledge and they were about to be returned to her. A second funeral was to be held the following month for his ashes and organs. I didn't want to ask anything else about it. The pain she felt was palpable and I had the impression that, although she appeared calm and in control, inside she was screaming.

●　　　●　　　●

I felt useless. I knew there was nothing I could do or say that could help so I didn't try. I did manage to say that my questionnaire seemed a bit irrelevant in the circumstances but she bailed me out by telling me it wasn't irrelevant and by insisting that I should go on. I took another look at her. There was a lot more to this woman than pain. There was pride and courage and kindness.

We finished the questionnaire and it was time to leave. I promised to ring Jo as soon as I got home (I couldn't wait to tell her all about it). I was sure that Jo would get in touch with Wendy straight away. I left, telling her that I would see her again.

'But next time I see you it won't be anything to do with work,' I told her. 'Next time I'll be seeing you as a friend.'

CHAPTER 2

Coming to Huddersfield

A couple of weeks later Wendy invited me round for tea. I was delighted to accept the invitation. We'd only spoken on the telephone since our meeting, and through Jo, who had, of course, called Wendy straight away.

In order to write this account, I asked Wendy to remind me what we had for tea that day. She remembered, of course, the woman has a memory that is more reliable than the one in my PC.

'We had quiche. Be sure to say that it wasn't just any old quiche,' she demanded. 'It was one of my home made quiches. It was lovely. I make a good quiche.'

Yes, now I remember the quiche. It was good. Wendy does, truthfully, make a very good quiche and that fact is now officially recorded here. Wendy-Lou had made buns, those nice little buns in individual paper cases with pink icing on. I felt honoured when I went in and saw somebody had made an effort just because I was coming to tea. I'm not particularly good at that sort of thing and my visitors often end up in the kitchen helping me out.

It felt better now that this wasn't work time. We were on comfortable terms and I was there by invitation. I admired the house. They'd obviously gone to a lot of trouble and effort with the painting and decorating. As before, everything was spick and span but it still looked comfortable. I didn't feel worried about creasing a cushion or dropping my fork. She smiled proudly and described what a mess it was in when she had first arrived. She hadn't seen the inside until the day she moved in because it was shuttered-up when she viewed it and accepted the tenancy. It was that sort of area. Some people have described it as 'rough'.

There are a lot of really lovely, decent people who live in that area and they get fed up of the bad reputation it has earned. It has earned its bad reputation, though. There were some families in that area who made life a misery for others. Then, when a house became vacant, they broke in and took whatever they could remove. The council had to fasten horrible shutters to the doors and windows of vacant properties. Part of the estate was due for demolition. Not because the houses were uninhabitable, they were good houses and surrounded by open fields and beautiful beech woodland. It was part of a plan to change the image of the area because it had become so hard to let the houses. Many local people would refuse to even consider moving there. With a high number of vacant properties, all boarded-up and awaiting demolition, it looked like a war zone.

●　　　●　　　●

'How come you moved to Huddersfield, Wendy?' I asked. 'I mean, I know why you left Wales, but why Huddersfield?'

She thought for a minute. Wendy has a precise mind. She doesn't just remember things - she remembers them in chronological order. She usually supplies dates, times and exact locations. She wasn't trying to remember, she was just wondering where to begin.

'After my William was murdered the whole family fell apart. My husband, Brian, started drinking. He'd always had a few but he started drinking really heavily. He got violent. William was the eldest. Next came Marc. Marc seemed to cope best out of all of us. He had a place of his own and kept himself working. He's married now, with two babies of his own. The next one down is Christopher. He started getting into trouble with the police. He was in and out of prison. He's in prison now. Wendy-Lou started going about with people who took drugs and began taking drugs herself. She got a flat of her own. I went through the Women's Refuge. I just couldn't take the drinking and the violence any more. I rented a little house in Newtown, just on my own. In no time at all I'd lost them. We'd been a family with a mum and a dad and four kids. We'd been happy. Then, there I was, all on my own. One night, about seven o'clock, I went to the Spar shop to get a packet of fags and a magazine to read. On my way I walked past the bank and there was someone asleep on that bench in front of it. I thought what it a shame it was to see them like that. On my way back I walked past the bench again and had another look. It was our Wendy-Lou! She was spark out on the bench. Anything could have happened to her'.

Wendy had already lost one of her kids and said that she did not want to lose another.

'Not again, not ever again ... I went over and picked her up and carried her back to my house. She hardly weighed anything, anyway. I put her on the sofa when I got back. I could see she was breathing alright so I left her to sleep it off. I was thinking to myself that I had to get her away from Wales. I had to get away and I had to take her with me. I looked for the fags I'd bought. I had dumped the bit of shopping on the table when I got in. They were there, where I'd left them. The magazine was there as well but it was open on a page with an article about relocating to Huddersfield. The headline was "Room to Breathe" and it was a story about a woman called Pauline and her family. Pauline and her husband had five kids and they lived on the eighth floor of a tower block in East London. They had relocated to Huddersfield through the Kirklees Council Relocation Scheme and had been allocated a four bedroom house in Deighton. Apparently there were houses to let immediately. There was a number to ring. I rang it straight away. I got through to an answering machine and left my details. The application pack came in the post, not the following morning but the morning after that. I filled it in and went down to the Health Council with it.'

Wendy explained that she had received support from the Health Council in Newtown and that they knew what she had gone through in the last five years. She had received incredible support both from the original chief officer and from the next one, who was appointed when the first one moved to another job. The Chief Officer wrote a statement, briefly outlining the circumstances, to support Wendy's application for accommodation in Huddersfield .

'I sent off the application and the next week I received an offer. Marc drove me up to Huddersfield to look at this house. It was dark and the house was all shuttered up. Our Marc begged me not to take it. I had to get away though. I had to get away from all the pain and the anger and the frustration. I had to get our Wendy away as well'.

She had moved in on May 28. It was the anniversary of William's first funeral.

'I didn't see the inside of the house until I moved into it. When I did, it was horrible. It was a disgrace, an absolute disgrace. It's been hard work getting it like this.'

'Well you've done a fantastic job of it,' I told her, looking round at her front room. 'It's a big house, as well, isn't it?'

'Yes. I told them I want our Christopher to come and live here when he comes out of prison. I'm trying to get some of my family back together again. Do you want a look round?'

I took the grand tour, admiring her hard work. It was a lot easier to talk about the nice carpets than talk about what she'd been through. I was thinking about it, though. I was also thinking about another Jo, the comedian Jo Brand. I'd been to see her show in Huddersfield the previous autumn. She'd read a copy of our local newspaper, the *Huddersfield Examiner,* and used the contents as part of her performance. She had been particularly keen on one article. Our local council were advertising the fact that they had properties to rent, with immediate possession, in Deighton. These properties were being advertised in London to try and cut down on the number of vacant lets. They had emphasised the wide open spaces and the fact that there were some three and even some four bedroom homes. Jo Brand held the newspaper up and told the audience how nice it would be for all those people living in the overcrowded conditions of London boroughs to move to these large homes with gardens.

'Deighton sounds nice,' she intoned, with a sarcastic smile. 'Is Deighton nice?' Some of the laughter sounded tinged with embarrassment.

'Well' she repeated, louder, 'is Deighton nice?'

'NO!' shouted the audience.

'Well,' said Jo Brand, 'you're just taking the piss, then, aren't you?' We nearly cried from laughing at that one. It didn't seem so funny now.

I wondered if I ought to express an opinion to Wendy. It seemed best not to. What was I supposed to say? I decided to speak with caution.

'How do you find it round here? Is it alright?' I asked. 'Well,' she said, 'we keep ourselves to ourselves and I don't bother anybody. I thought it was alright until the burglary. I'm frightened to go anywhere now. I daren't leave the house unoccupied.'

Moving to Huddersfield had been a lot easier for me. It had been a home-coming. I had friends and family to come home to. They had been there to give me support and encouragement when times were tough. There had been some difficulties at first. I'd signed a six month contract to rent a damp little house and when it was up we got notice to quit because the owner had decided to sell it. I'd taken advice from a Housing Advisory Service, who had been very helpful. Because I was on benefits at the time, my furniture had been taken into storage. We were housed in temporary accommodation until I was offered a local authority house to rent. I had been allowed to specify which areas were acceptable to me. The advice from the advisory service had been to only put down those areas where I felt I wanted to live. It might mean waiting longer to be housed, but it would be worth it in the end because I would then be able to settle down and make a permanent home in an area where I was happy. Deighton hadn't been one of the areas I was willing to accept. We'd been lucky and were offered a three bedroom home on the edge of a quiet estate within a relatively short time. The house hadn't been shuttered when it was empty. Houses in the area where I live don't stay empty for very long and are safe enough between tenants.

●   ●   ●

There seemed to be something wrong with housing the vulnerable and unwary in a place where they may not be safe. These women had been through enough already. Wendy's application would have been quite informative about her circumstances, especially with a supporting statement from the chief officer of the Health Council of Wales to accompany it.

I worried about them. I hoped nothing else happened. I hoped we weren't just taking the piss.

CHAPTER 3

Knock On the Door

Jo had promised to visit and it was only a week or two later when she did. We were invited to Wendy's house for the day. She said that she and Wendy-Lou loved cooking and they didn't have enough visitors. Jo arrived at my house one Friday evening. I was learning to drive and had taken the decision to do the driving. I had been preparing for this terrifying journey with my driving instructor, who had kindly taken me on a practice run. I found learning to drive to be the hardest thing I had ever done. Obtaining a degree was more interesting, more fun and a whole lot easier and less dangerous.

Jo was her usual encouraging self on the way up there, quite early on the Saturday morning. It was a straightforward journey and nothing untoward happened. This did not stop me from sitting upright, my nose about six inches away from the windscreen, clutching at the steering wheel until my knuckles turned white. Being able to drive was one thing, not being afraid of doing it was something I had yet to master. Wendy and Wendy-Lou were generous in their praise when Jo told them I had driven really well. Jo didn't mention the white knuckles. I would have enjoyed the cries of 'Well done!' and 'See, you can do it!' so much more if I hadn't been so painfully aware that I had to drive home again at the end of the day.

They had shopped, baked, prepared vegetables for cooking and cleaned. The dining table had been brought out into one half of the big front room and polished until it gleamed. The kettle went on and tea and cakes were brought to us. We couldn't have felt more welcome.

Wendy laughed as she told Jo that when I first arrived she thought that I had been sent from Wales to shut her up. I had been one more official coming to visit her. When I had arrived that very first time she had gone into the kitchen to put the kettle on. She heard me talking to Wendy-Lou and heard me mention Wales. Her first thought was that I had been sent to silence her, until she heard me go on to say that all the evidence pointed to there being two killers responsible for the murders. That wasn't the official line. She had come out of the kitchen to see what I had to say. When I had said that I was a friend of Jo's she couldn't believe it. Jo had always listened to her, believed her and supported her. Jo was on her side. If I was a friend of Jo's, I must be an ally.

Jo laughed back and assured her that I was quite trustworthy. She then went on to explain that Wendy had made some very serious complaints and had refused to let them drop. 'What complaints?' I wanted to know, remembering now that I had initially been advised not to visit her because she had made a complaint against Victim Support in Wales.

'Well' said Wendy, 'Everything that could go wrong did go wrong. We received terrible treatment after William was murdered. I don't want that to happen to any other family. I had to speak out about it. I want the system changed. I'm fighting the system.' I needed to understand what had gone wrong for Wendy and her family if I was going to understand her fight. It was time for her to open up. She didn't just remember her past, she re-visited it. I knew that it was going to be tough for her to talk about it, especially as she kept tight control over her emotions as she talked.

Wendy-Lou escaped to her room to listen to music when she sensed that Wendy was about to begin. It was probably difficult for her to listen, both because it was her own traumatic past and also because watching her mother courageously describe the events would be painful. I was a little apprehensive, too. Over the course of the day, between cups of tea, Wendy told some of her story.

●　　　●　　　●

It was on Thursday, 2 May 1996, at half past eight in the morning - a beautiful day with the sun already shining. Marc lived not far away in his own flat. Christopher had left early to do his paper round before school and Wendy-Lou had just got off to school half an hour earlier. William was in rehab in Cardiff. He had been through a difficult time. He had got in with a wrong crowd and started taking drugs, got into trouble for shoplifting and then breached court orders and finished up in even deeper trouble. Eventually, he had attended court and the magistrates had given him a choice. He could either go to prison or he could sort himself out and attend rehab. It wasn't a difficult choice for William because he had got to the point where he wanted to sort himself out. He had been in rehab nearly six months and was due to come home in two weeks. For the whole time he was there, he had stayed clean and responded really well. He had been happy and positive about everything when I had spoken to him on the 'phone the week before. At eighteen years old he seemed to be growing up - and I was proud of how he was doing.

There was a knock on the door and Brian went to answer it. I heard a man's voice ask to speak to 'Wendy', so I went to the door too. The sun lit up two figures standing on the doorstep. There were two police officers in uniform. One was a sergeant and the younger one was a PC. They looked serious, unsmiling. I knew immediately that something was wrong. My first thought was that something had happened to Christopher, maybe he had been knocked down while he was doing his paper round. The sergeant asked us to go and sit down.

I was filled with a sense of dread. I could feel myself trembling as I made my way to the sofa, wondering what I was about to hear. We sat on the sofa and he got down on one knee in front of us so that his eyes were on a level with ours. He said there had been an incident in Llandrindod Wells involving William and that he had been stabbed.

It was like being hit, a sudden attack out of nowhere. I felt my stomach churn and contract - I had to run to the bathroom to be sick.

I stayed in the bathroom to wipe my face and gather my thoughts. This was not real. I was in the safety of my own bathroom. William was in Cardiff. The sun was shining. This *could not* be real. I went back downstairs but the two police officers were still there. I could not persuade myself that it was just a mad hallucination when I could see both of them right there in front of me. The sergeant spoke again. I could feel his concern and both were respectful. I knew they were giving us the information in the kindest way possible, but the news was so unacceptable that I wished them gone. I wanted them to go and the message to go with them. I wanted it to be a mistake, or a dream or lie. The sergeant said that they had the Victim Support co-ordinator, John Hedges, with them and asked if he could come in.

One of us must have said 'Yes' because he went to the door and in John Hedges came. He was a big man with a beard, wearing a short-sleeved white shirt and navy blue trousers. He came towards me and made a movement to grab me and give me a hug. I moved away and held my hands out in front of me to keep him back. I certainly didn't want this man hugging me. I didn't want *anybody* to touch me. My every muscle and every bone were hurting. I couldn't bear the pain of being touched. I realised that none of my children were in the house. They had to know that something had happened to William. I needed them here, needed to gather them in. I told the police officers that they had to go and tell Marc. They had to let Christopher and Wendy-Lou know. They seemed to understand me, even though I could hardly understand myself. The sergeant spoke some words that I couldn't comprehend and both officers turned to leave. John Hedges spoke. He had a rough voice with a Welsh accent. He said that the police had gone to tell Marc what had happened and that he would take Brian to the school to tell Christopher and Wendy-Lou. I understood that. I understood it as I watched the door close behind them, leaving me alone with this impossible nightmare.

After the door closed, a silence filled the house. I'd just heard that William had been stabbed. I didn't know what to do. I couldn't just stand there. I started cleaning the kitchen worktops. I have no idea why I did that. I just started cleaning them. As I rubbed away at the worktops I felt a pain overcome me. I fell to the floor, on to my hands and knees, puking-up in agony. The light disappeared, I was in a darkened world and a great wrenching pain was tearing at my gut. From somewhere above my head I could hear sinister, guttural sounds. The noises echoed my own pain but were bestial, the appalling sounds of an animal in agony. I wished the noise would stop. It was some while before I realised that the sounds were coming from me.

I don't know for how long I was there, but I heard the door opening and I managed to look to see who it was. It was Marc and Christopher. They looked terrible. They were ashen, shocked. I knew I had to pull myself together for them. I told them to come in and sit down but they didn't, they just stood in the hallway, silent. I was still trying to persuade them to come and sit down when Brian and Wendy-Lou arrived with John Hedges. Wendy-Lou ran to me and just threw herself into my arms. I hugged her for a minute or two and then went to put the kettle on. It was all I could think of doing.

When the boys managed to speak, they explained that Christopher had called in to see Marc before he went to school. The police had found them both at the flat and told them that their brother was dead and they needed to go home. The message had not been given unkindly, but the shock had left them with only the bare bones of the news.

The phone started to ring and John Hedges said that he had to answer it because he had been instructed to do so by the police. He did, and I could hear the voice of my sister at the other end. She was crying. He gave the phone to me and my sister said she would come round as soon as she could. She just kept sobbing and saying that it was terrible.

Hedges' mobile started ringing. He answered it, talked for a while and then told us that he had to go. He said that there had been a robbery and someone had pinched a woman's handbag. He had to go and deal with it. At the time it seemed to me that he was full of his own importance and I was glad when he left the house. Right then I just didn't care what had happened to anybody else. I didn't want to know about the robbery. I was trying to take in what had happened to my son. This is how it was with John Hedges. He was not a wicked man. Essentially he was (and is) a good man. He's large, convivial and loud. That was just what I didn't need at this time. To be fair, John Hedges probably did not expect to have to deal with a murder case. He wasn't prepared to come face to face with such trauma. Neither was I. That is how murder is. It is indiscriminate and unexpected. It came round to my house that morning and skinned me alive, leaving my every nerve sensitive to each movement in the air. John Hedges met a woman who was raw, agonised and his every movement, his every word seemed clumsy to me. He hid from our pain by making himself busy. Did he want to run away from the situation? I know I did.

It was only then that I noticed Trisha. She was a Victim Support volunteer. Apparently John Hedges had taken her to the school so that she could be with Wendy-Lou when they told her about William. Trisha was quite different. I sensed that she was a kind woman. We had a cup of tea and I didn't mind her being there. She stayed for about an hour and then she said that she realised we needed to have some time to ourselves. My sister had arrived and she wanted to leave us all together for a bit of privacy.

By now I was desperate to see William. I had bits of information. William had been in Llandod. William had been stabbed. William was dead. It didn't make sense. William was in Cardiff. I had to go and see him. Whatever had happened to him, wherever he was, I needed to be with him. The telephone rang again. I was able to answer it myself now that John Hedges was no longer answering the calls. The call was from the police to tell me that they had left a message for my brother, who was away in Germany, in the army. This seemed strange. They were going to enormous efforts to let all the family know that something had happened but I didn't really know what that something was yet. It was all just words. I hadn't seen William. He might be in Cardiff. Someone might have made a mistake.

It wasn't long before John Hedges came back again. He started talking about the robbery. I didn't understand why he was talking about what *he* had been doing. I didn't care what he had been doing in the couple of hours that he had been gone. I didn't care about *him*. I just wanted to see *William*. I kept interrupting him to tell him this and asking him to take me to William. Eventually he said that he would ring the police to see what was happening, but his mobile 'phone started ringing again. He took the call and then said that he had to go because there had been an accident on the by-pass and someone had been killed. I was astounded when he left. I needed to see William. I didn't know where he was. Why didn't somebody tell me where he was? It had been hours and hours since that first knock on the door and still I didn't know what was happening.

We sat again, then stood, then paced up and down. We were all in shock and waiting for something. The day seemed to be lasting forever.

•   •   •

The telephone rang again. This time Brian answered it. He listened for a minute and then put it down. I saw his face and it looked as though something had suddenly snapped. Something like a string, holding his features together, had suddenly snapped and his face had slumped. He walked over to the banisters and grabbed them. He pulled on them so hard that the handrail came off in his hands as he started screaming. It was a while before he could tell us what had been said. The call had been from the police officer who was to be the family liaison officer, from Llandod. He had said 'The body is ready to be moved now. Do you want to get the undertaker or shall we?'

When I managed to get that information out of Brian, I called the police. I only had the number for Newtown Police Station, but I rang it anyway. I spoke to whichever officer answered and tried to explain what had been said to Brian but at first he didn't understand. I must have been incoherent. He said, 'What body? What body are you talking about?' Eventually I made him understand and he was very apologetic. I told him that I had to see William. He promised to make a couple of calls and then ring back to talk to me.

I was waiting for him to call me back when there was a knock on the door and John Hedges was back again. He came in and started to tell us about the accident on the by-pass. I wanted to scream. How could he possibly think that we could be interested in this story? Could he not see what a state we were all in? I interrupted him and told him about the telephone calls. I told him that I wanted to know where my William was. I asked why I couldn't see him. I was insistent. He took out his mobile telephone and made a call. He finished the call and said that the police would ring him back.

It wasn't long before our landline rang. Hedges got to it and answered it before anyone else did. He was speaking quietly into the telephone, almost whispering. Eventually he put the 'phone down and said that William had been taken to the hospital in Hereford and that he would take us to see him.

My sister took the children with her. They shuffled off like zombies, all four of them.

●   ●   ●

Brian sat in the front, next to John Hedges and I sat in the back of his cramped little car. The drive seemed to take forever, although it is less than fifty miles. Eventually, he pulled into the car park at the front of the hospital. He told us that he would go and find the mortuary and that we should wait by the car until he came back for us. I didn't want to wait any longer. I couldn't wait any longer. I had no choice, though and we stood waiting in the car park, while the world carried on around us as though nothing had happened. After nearly an hour I refused to wait any longer. I told Brian that we should go and find the mortuary ourselves. We went into the hospital. We had no idea where anything was so we just wandered around until we came to a reception desk. I went up to the desk and asked where the mortuary was.

The woman behind the desk asked who we were with so I explained about the Victim Support co-ordinator, John Hedges and how we had waited for him for nearly an hour. She asked us to wait for a moment while she went to ring the mortuary but I couldn't stand still. I felt as if I was going to explode or faint, or something. I had to keep moving, so we wandered off. We were in a busy corridor about five minutes later when we bumped into John Hedges. He said out loud, 'The body is not ready to be viewed yet so we'll go and have a cup of tea and wait.'

I saw people look round. I didn't want their eyes on me. I was like an animal in pain, unable to cope with people and their interested stares. John Hedges set off and we followed. I expected to be taken into some little side room where we could be private and I could hide from all the curious eyes. He walked us back to the car and ushered us in. I was completely baffled. He drove to Safeway and pulled into the supermarket car park. I was at a complete loss when he got out of the car. As I got out, I said, 'What are we doing here?' He said that we were just going to go and have a drink. I was sure now that William was alive. If William were dead, we wouldn't be taken to a supermarket. I started to believe that someone had made a terrible mistake.

We went into the cafe and he told me to go and sit down while he and Brian went to get the drinks. As they went off, I saw John Hedges speaking to Brian and Brian reacting in a horrified manner. I wondered what Brian had heard. I wondered what they were keeping from me. William was my son and it felt like there were some awful secrets being kept. I had been waiting all day to see him, just waiting and waiting. Now I was in a supermarket cafe and John Hedges was muttering horrible secrets to my husband. When they came over with the drinks I asked what was happening. I couldn't tell what they said but I knew that they were just trying to keep me calm. I started to weep. I sat in a supermarket cafe with people all around me while I wept. There were babies crying and tills ringing and all the usual hustle and bustle. It was tea-time by now and the supermarket was busy. I felt isolated, alienated and on view to the world. The world had gone mad, or I was going mad. I could not possibly be sitting in a supermarket cafe waiting to view the body of my murdered son. This wouldn't happen to anybody. Something else must be happening, something horrible, unthinkable. Perhaps I wasn't really there, perhaps I had gone mad and none of this was real. All these thoughts spun around in my head as I sat there losing touch with my sanity. Around me, people wandered past with trays of tea and food. I felt their eyes, like question marks, cutting into my flesh. It was like a punishment, a public whipping. I hid my face in my hands and made a picture of my son. I could see his smiling face.

• • •

Eventually John Hedges sat and looked at his watch and said that we should go. He took us into the mortuary department and into a little side room. It had a table and chairs. There were three doors in the room. A police officer was in there. He was in uniform but not wearing his hat. He had a kind face and spoke gently to us. He introduced himself as Sergeant Price but said we should call him by his first name, Robert. It was time to see William. John Hedges said, 'Are you ready for this?' I murmured to Brian 'How could anyone be ready for this?'

Suddenly the door was opened into the mortuary. A smell, like that of school chemistry laboratories assailed me, reminding me of Bunsen burners and smouldering chemicals in test tubes. There was a trolley in there and on it a twisted body, covered up to the chin in a dark purple sheet, knees bent to one side, shoulders and head flat with the face pointing towards the ceiling. The mouth was slightly open, revealing the teeth. I recognised the teeth - William's teeth. This was William, laid on a trolley in a mortuary. I stepped back, horrified and Brian dropped to the floor. The door to the mortuary was pushed shut as I moved to another of the doors in the side room and tried to get out. This door was locked, I couldn't open it. I just stood pressing myself to the door, trying to hide my face. I didn't want to see this. I didn't want it to be true. John Hedges grabbed hold of my arm. He said, 'You can't identify him like that. You've got to go in.'

Brian got to his feet and Hedges grabbed him with his other hand and pulled us towards the door. Sergeant Price opened it again. Hedges pulled us right into the mortuary and the door was closed behind us. I saw William again. There was a huge swelling on the left side of his face, right from his nose to his cheekbone. It was a pure white swelling. His eyes were closed but there was still a look of horror on his contorted face. The gold ring was missing from his eyebrow and the stud from his ear. Stripped of his familiar jewellery, he looked so naked and vulnerable. I wondered why he wasn't flat on the trolley. Instead his knees were bent to one side so that he looked twisted. This was not a body relaxed in death. The sheet was pulled to one side by his bent knees and revealed a hand. I looked at his hand. It seemed to be the wrong colour and the ring was missing from his finger. He was stripped of everything and lay there, gripped in that last moment of horror. I couldn't touch him. I whispered to Brian, 'Kiss him for me'. Brian moved to William and bent down to kiss him but the mortuary assistant standing by the trolley pushed him off and said, 'You can't touch him, you'll contaminate the evidence and the body is infected.'

Afterwards, we staggered back into the side room. Sergeant Price wanted some details, like William's date of birth, and we had to sign the identification form. He asked us the questions kindly. He asked us if we knew Fiona. We had never met Fiona but William had talked about her. William had been required to attend the Mid-Wales Hospital in Talgarth for an assessment before entering rehab. It was there that he had met Fiona, who was being treated for ME and its accompanying depression. They had become close friends and kept in touch. I vaguely wondered what this had to do with Fiona.

'Fiona is dead, too,' said Sgt. Price, 'we have someone in custody. He handed himself in.'

As we stood there answering questions I heard the trolley being wheeled, I heard the noise of William being put into the fridge and I heard the fridge door close on him.

'How many times was he stabbed?' I asked, realising I hadn't seen his body.

Sergeant Price looked sad. 'He was stabbed about ten times,' he said, gently. He gave us some telephone numbers and said that we could call if we needed anything. Just then another police officer came into the side room from one of the other doors and said, 'Doctor and Mrs. Ovis have arrived, get the Cromptons out quick.' With that he rushed us out of the side entrance, almost pushing us out. We were directed to leave by the back door. I suddenly felt that I was in the wrong, being hustled out by the back entrance made me feel that I had no right to be near my son.

John Hedges drove us home. I knew I hadn't said goodbye to my son and now I was leaving him behind with a look of horror on his face. Now I just wanted to soothe that horror from him. I wanted to take him in my arms and make it better. John Hedges said that we would be able to say goodbye to him properly in the Chapel of Rest.

● ● ●

When we arrived home there were people waiting outside, strangers. One was trying to take photos of us. They said they were from the local press. They called to us and asked us to talk to them, look at them. We just rushed into the house and I collapsed onto the sofa, weeping.

I telephoned my sister to let her know we were back. I said very little to her, just that we were back and that it *was* William. My sister returned with the children and they went up to bed, saying hardly anything. Marc stayed over. He couldn't be alone on this night.

I couldn't go up to bed. Brian and I sat downstairs all night. Sometimes we talked and sometimes cried. Brian told me that he had known it was William before he went in. That was what John Hedges had said to him while they were getting the drinks in the Safeway cafe. He had told Brian that he had been to see the body and it *was* that of William. In the middle of my trauma, little angry, unforgiving knots were beginning to form. I didn't like the way John Hedges had behaved. I thought that he had been like a voyeur with authority. I wouldn't forget it. I didn't like the way the police officer had spoken to Brian on the telephone, or bundled us out of the side room and through the back entrance at the mortuary. And what was it that mortuary assistant had said? Not allowed to kiss him goodbye? Infected? That was my son he was talking about. I wouldn't forget that, either.

CHAPTER 4

Carry the Flowers

The next morning I received a call from the police. I was required to go Llandrindod Wells Police Station and make a Life Statement. When Brian and I arrived, he rang the bell at the front desk. A woman police constable came to the desk, glanced at us, said, 'Wait a minute' then walked away. We waited and waited. I was becoming increasingly anxious and Brian could see that I was feeling unwell. A man came in. He was a portly, well-dressed man who looked like a solicitor. He heard me asking Brian how much longer I would have to wait. Stepping forward, he looked at us both as though we were beneath contempt. He curled his lip slightly as he snapped, 'Just wait, will you? They are busy. Don't you know there has been a double murder in this town?'

Anger gave me back my strength.

'Yes, I am aware of that fact. One of the victims is my son,' I replied - staring angrily into his over-fed face. I saw his expression change in an instant. It was as if I had slapped him. I was glad. I had plenty of pain to share around. He was welcome to some of it.

•   •   •

Eventually we were taken upstairs by one of the investigating officers. We sat in a small interview room and the officer in charge entered, briefly introduced himself, and then said, 'Crompton was a little shit anyway. You're lucky it happened here and not in South Wales or you wouldn't even have got an investigation.'

Any strength I had found was quickly lost again as I gave the statement. This officer had decided that William was better dead than alive and made sure I was aware of his opinion. Each comment he threw at me landed like a blow. I took it like a beating, too overwhelmed for tears, too crippled to vocalise any defence. The Life Statement I gave described my boy, truthfully, as someone who had been troubled by problems and who had rebelled in his early teens. He had been punished for some of that behaviour, but it never included violence of any kind. He had realised what a mess he was making of his life and gratefully accepted the chance to sort himself out when he was offered the option of attending a rehab unit. He had successfully engaged with the rigours of the course, received excellent reports and was looking to the future with enthusiasm. The last time I had seen him, just a month before his death, he seemed healthy and happy. I was proud of the change in him and told him so. He had a new-found confidence. He was enjoying a sense of achievement, the good reports and the praise. Once I saw that he had turned his life around, I finally stopped feeling anxious about him. I believed that he was going to be alright. He was just eighteen years old with his life in front of him.

I had seen a glimpse of the man he was going to be - tall, handsome, full of energy and facing the future with a happy smile. Now I would never see the man he would have grown to be. Instead I sat in that interview room and took the spiteful comments from this cynical, case-hardened police officer who saw a young lad with a record as the scum of the earth. But that young lad was mine and he was dead, so I took the abuse like a beating in his place and understood at last why William had complained to me about the brutality of certain police officers. I now saw the same kind of attitudes being displayed. William seemed to have had a fair point when he said that some of them were unfit for their profession.

After the Life Statement had been given I was seen by Sergeant Price. He explained that the officer who had bundled us out of the mortuary was no longer working on the case. It was intended that the officer would be our family liaison officer but now it was Sergeant Price who was to fill that role. He would now be our contact. I was grateful for this news. It was the first time Sergeant Price had undertaken that role, but he seemed to have an instinct for it. Throughout this whole nightmare I met people that I could trust and they never let me down. He was the first of such people and it is those people I remember most. Without them, I feel that I couldn't have survived. I felt it was inappropriate to tell him my opinion of the previous officer and, anyway, I would have been unable to repeat his cruel words without breaking into floods of uncontrollable tears. I did say that he had told me that the murderer made a tape-recording of the murders and that I never wanted to hear it. I would not wish to hear my son breathing his last.

Sergeant Price assured me that he had heard the tape. There was some music on it, by Meat Loaf, and some background noises but it was not a recording of the sounds made by William and Fiona as they died. He also told me a little more about Fiona. She was the daughter of Dr and Mrs. Ovis. Dr Ovis was a local GP. He was not able to tell me much more at that time, but I was relieved to speak to this decent, kind man before I left the building.

•   •   •

The days that followed were filled with pain. A post mortem was carried out on William. I knew it had to be done but the thought of my boy being cut open like that filled me with horror. Sergeant Price telephoned to tell me that a second post mortem was to be carried out at the instigation of the defence. I wailed in anguish. What could they possibly find out now? My boy had been through enough. Now the representatives of his killer were carving him up again. It was the third time William's body would be mutilated. This should not be done for the benefit of the man who stabbed him to death.

I begged Sergeant Price not to let them do it. He could do nothing to prevent it, but promised that he would telephone me when it was over. He kept his promise. He told me that it had been carried out with the greatest of respect. 'Like an operation,' he said. It was some small comfort and I kept his words with me. I felt that someone was watching out for William.

I could think about little else but the murder during the long days that followed. My mind created pictures of the killings. I wondered how long William and Fiona had suffered. I wondered about the killer. What did he look like? He was just a shadowy figure in my nightmares. Often during those nightmares, I was wide awake.

We needed to say a proper goodbye to William. I wanted to have him home for one night, before the funeral. I wanted him to make his last journey from our house, from a place where he was loved. We had no money but that didn't matter. I'd do whatever it took to give my boy a decent funeral. I would have him buried with dignity and with love. John Hedges contacted an undertaker for us who paid us a visit to discuss the arrangements. I made an effort to tidy myself up, to start thinking straight. I needed to be able to concentrate properly when he arrived. This was important.

There was a knock at the door and a small man in a dark suit was ushered in. He was the undertaker. For a funeral director, it seemed to me that he showed a distinct lack of respect. He knew we had no money and told us so. He said that we couldn't afford a burial. I was furious and said, 'We're having one'. I wanted my William to have a decent burial and that is what he was going to have. He said that the body was infected and would have to be cremated. This information, he assured us, had come from Hereford Hospital. I was astounded. How could his body be infected? He'd been stabbed to death - there was nothing infectious about it.

While I was still reeling with shock, the undertaker left, turning to tell us that we couldn't have flowers either because of the cost. I went to the benefits office and asked for a grant to bury William but they refused point blank. I was told that in due course I would be receiving some money under the Criminal Injuries Compensation Scheme, so that I should take out a loan against that instead. So twenty-five pounds per week was deducted from our normal benefits to cover the repayments. It would be difficult to handle but my priorities were different now - money didn't seem that important.

A few days later the undertaker came round to our house again. He wanted the money up front. 'No money, no funeral,' he told us. He presented his bill. I was shocked to see that he was charging us for the transportation of William's body from Llandod to Hereford. I argued, I told him that he couldn't charge us for that. We hadn't organized it. He said he would contact the coroner and see if he would waive the fee. He insisted on the rest of the money, though. We hadn't been able to borrow the whole amount. We had saved as much as we could. With our savings and the loan we were eighty-three pounds short. He took the money. The undertaker became known as 'The Bloodsucker' in our house and was soon shortened to BS. 'Bloodsucker by name and Bloodsucker by nature' became a familiar saying.

Before leaving he told us that we couldn't have the coffin in our house before the funeral. William's body had decomposed and the coffin had been sealed in Hereford. This hit me like a physical attack. I wanted to see William and kiss him goodbye. Marc, Christopher and Wendy-Lou were having difficulty accepting that William was dead and needed to see him. Now I knew that none of us would ever see him again.

●   ●   ●

My family arrived for the funeral. I wanted pall bearers to carry William into the crematorium. We had ordered flowers from the florist. Everybody was turned out in their best suits. We were determined that we would give William a dignified send off. My brother Bill reminded BS that he, our brother John, his friend Alan, Brian and Brian's brothers would carry the coffin. BS said that it would have to go on a trolley. The handles were not weight-bearing and it couldn't be lifted. Bill tried to make him change his mind and it was brewing into an argument. Bill seemed to realise this and backed off.

We got into the cars and left. We drove to the crematorium. As we were travelling on the by-pass, Bill overtook the funeral cars. He drove through the gates of the crematorium, just far enough up the drive to allow the other cars in, and there he stopped his car, blocking the drive. He got out of the driver's seat and approached the hearse. BS got out and Bill looked down at him. 'We are going to carry this coffin,' he told the undertaker and organized the coffin bearers, who marched to the back of the hearse. BS must have realised he had met his match. He was outnumbered and nobody was prepared to enter into any discussion with him about it. The coffin was lifted onto the shoulders of friends and family. They would take the weight and not rely on the handles.

'And YOU, little man. I've got a job for you. Carry the flowers,' Bill said to BS, thrusting the floral 'WILLIAM' into his hands.

I love Bill. That day he was my hero. But it was a pity my hero was not familiar with the crematorium. How was he to know that the drive went on forever? For fifteen minutes they carried William on their shoulders. They didn't stop, not once. They did me proud. I did notice, though, that as they turned the last two corners, their steps had become slower and slower.

BS told us that we would be informed by the staff of the crematorium when the ashes were ready for collection. Eventually I asked John Hedges to make enquiries. He found out for us that the undertaker had told the crematorium to release the ashes to him. He said that he would let us have them when we had paid our bill in full! I knew he kept coffins and the like in his garage and I hated thinking of William's ashes in amongst them. I wanted the remains of my boy back and they were being held to ransom. It took us ages to save up that money. What with money already being deducted from our benefits each week, it was tough. But we finally made it, paid up and demanded William back. When the ashes arrived they were in a large brown plastic jar. I was furious. I had ordered an oak casket and they had arrived in what looked like a catering-size HP Sauce bottle.

I spoke to BS and he said that the casket was not included in the price. We would have to pay more if we wanted it. It was the final straw. I went to a solicitor and it was only then sorted out. I finally had William's ashes in a decent oak casket - but I had to fight tooth and nail to get there. There was something wrong about everything. I shouldn't have had to fight. Another knot formed itself inside of me.

This was something else I would remember.

CHAPTER 5

A Date for the Trial

I decided that I needed to lay some flowers on the place where William had died. He and Fiona had been in a bungalow that had belonged to her grandmother. She was about to move into the bungalow and had started transferring some of her own things there. Either her grandmother had died or moved elsewhere, I didn't know which. Apparently, someone called Andrew Cole had broken into the bungalow during the early hours and murdered them there. I made a telephone call to Sergeant Price and asked him if he would ask Dr and Mrs. Ovis if I could possibly go there to lay some flowers. He asked for my permission to give them my telephone number and I readily agreed.

The next day Mrs. Ovis rang me. She invited me to the bungalow and we arranged to meet in Llandod. Brian drove us over there. I imagined that there would be a macabre atmosphere in that place and so did Brian. He didn't really want to go there and we felt that it would not be right for the children so he took them to the lake in Llandod while my sister, Sue and I went to meet Mrs. Ovis, our arms filled with flowers.

●　　●　　●

We entered the bungalow through the back door that led into the kitchen. Sue held my hand as we stepped inside. My stomach did somersaults, I didn't know what to expect. We walked through the kitchen and into the living room. The rooms were small and it felt like the home of an elderly person. In the living room was a cottage style three piece suite that definitely spoke more of an old lady than of a young person. Then I noticed the black stereo looking incongruous in the corner. I remembered the reference to the tape-recording and being told that there was loud music playing when Andrew Cole came to the bungalow that night. Another door of the room was ajar and I realised that it led into a bedroom. My stomach lurched and my heart skipped a beat. William and Fiona had been murdered there and I was looking across into the very room.

My steps felt heavy as I moved towards the bedroom door. I stepped inside, and – nothing! I felt nothing at all. The room was empty and the carpet had been removed, leaving just the underlay still tacked to the floor. I can't remember what was covering the walls but there were certainly no bloodstains. Neither was there a smell of paint to indicate that it had recently been redecorated. It was a small bedroom with just this one door between it and the living room. I remembered hearing that Cole had broken in through the window but the window wasn't broken so it must have been fixed. I tried to send out an antenna in order to feel the horror that had happened here. No remnants of that night, no confirmation of the brutal killings were detectable. I was relieved not to feel the residue of that horror, but confused. This was an empty space. My son was gone. I could find nothing of him here.

I was probably only in the room for a few minutes but it felt like hours. I wondered where to put the flowers and Mrs. Ovis said that she would get a vase to put them in. We left the bedroom and walked down a corridor towards the bathroom. There was another door open and I could see that this was the box room, literally full of stored boxes, and a single bed. I wondered why the door was open. I vaguely thought that I would have had the door tightly shut so that visitors could not see into my storage area. Then I realised why all the doors were open. There were no door handles on any of the internal doors. I was forming questions to ask about the door handles and whether the bungalow had been decorated. I looked towards Mrs Ovis to ask but as I saw her face I realised that she was concentrating on controlling her emotions. I could see the struggle in her expression and recognised the grief in her eyes, as raw as my own. Of course, this bungalow belonged to her family. Perhaps they had been responsible for having the place cleaned, removing the stains. Perhaps she was remembering how this room was, just after the bodies had been removed and the evidence collected. Perhaps they burned the carpet and the bed. It was a brave and kind thing she was doing this day. How could I ask her what had been cleaned away? I could not bring myself to ask her anything.

She drove us back into Llandod and we talked in the car. I wanted to go there on the first anniversary of William and Fiona's deaths. She agreed that we would be able to and suggested that we would go out for a meal together afterwards. We talked a little about what we were going through. We would both measure our lives by the same date from now on. There would be one year since our child died and then two years and three. For the rest of our lives we would march to the same funeral drum. It was during this conversation that she mentioned kissing Fiona goodbye in the mortuary. I turned my face away so that she would not see the sudden jealousy that briefly welled up inside me. So she had been allowed to kiss Fiona. She hadn't been physically pulled away from her child like Brian had when he had bent down to kiss William. Fiona had been kissed, William had not. A lump came into my throat as I filed this away with the other hurts that swam around in my vast ocean of pain.

●　　　●　　　●

The whole legal system presented nightmares. The first time I attended the magistrates' court was for the commital hearing. I just wanted to see the face of the killer. I could no longer bear the dark, shadowy face that my mind had created. It was becoming more and more monstrous. I needed a real face to replace it. A photograph of him had appeared in the local newspaper, *The Shropshire Star*, but he had a blanket over his face. I would have loved to have pulled that blanket off his face. There he was, protected from the public gaze. I didn't have a blanket to protect me when I sat in Safeway's cafe.

My sister and I arranged to meet John Hedges at court. I went in with her and we sat at the back, quietly for about one and a half hours. I saw people coming in to be dealt with for non-payment of fines and motoring offences. My sister and I grew more and more anxious, just wanting to see Andrew Cole and take our leave. Eventually the other cases were dealt with. John Hedges said that there would be a little wait and suggested that we go outside for a cigarette. I needed one by now, so we did. As we were about to go back in, Hedges approached us and said that there was a problem. Cole would not go into the courtroom if we were in there. We were therefore not allowed to go back in. I was furious. I really didn't care what the alleged killer wanted. He was the criminal, not us. I marched back into the building but was met by a group of people barring the way. John Hedges joined them. We were physically prevented from entering the courtroom.

Hedges told us to go into town for a coffee and come back in an hour or so. We had no choice but to leave. I couldn't believe that my wishes were being totally disregarded in order to make this killer more comfortable. It was a public building and I had every right to be there. I knew how to sit quietly and knew not to disrupt the proceedings. I would have overcome my feelings in order to sit with respect at the back of the courtroom and see the man who was charged with killing my son. But no, his wishes were to be granted, not mine. I felt that he had given up his right to take control of the situation when he took away my son's right to live. He should have been dragged into the court if he refused to enter with dignity.

It was a week or two before I rang John Hedges and let him know how angry and frustrated I was about being excluded from the court. I told him that I wanted to put a face to the name of Andrew Cole. He promised that he would take us to court because there was another hearing scheduled in Mold in a few weeks time.

Finally the day came around and Brian, Sue and I went with him to Mold. We went into the building and needed to find out what courtroom the case would be heard in, so made enquiries. When we gave our names I thought I could sense something change in the atmosphere. I had a strong feeling that our presence was causing disquiet and I felt eyes swivelling towards us. John Hedges had gone over to the entrance of a courtroom and I could see him in conversation with a woman. The woman came over to us and explained that she was representing the Crown Prosecution Service and that she was very sorry but we would be unable to enter the courtroom because it was a closed hearing involving an argument about medical records being released for the trial. Frustrated once again, we left. John Hedges admitted that when he had been given the news he had told her that she would have to go and tell us we would not be allowed in as he couldn't face giving us the news himself.

●   ●   ●

The trial date seemed to take forever to come around. It was scheduled for December and I was glad that it was going to be over before Christmas. Shortly before the due date we were contacted by the police to be informed that the trial had been rescheduled for January. Counsel for prosecution, who had all the papers, was now unable to continue with the case and had passed the papers to another, Martin Thomas QC - Lord Thomas of Gresford.

Christmas was very difficult. The children tried to recognise it. Christopher bought a tree and put it in the corner of the living room where it stayed, undecorated and ignored, until it went brown and the needles heaped up on the floor beneath it. We gave the children a small amount of money each and asked them to go out and buy some things for themselves. I remember that these items were wrapped and placed under the dying tree. I don't know who wrapped them, it wasn't me. Perhaps my poor children wrapped their own gifts. We were like shipmates on a small boat during a fierce storm, just clinging on and hoping to survive until the calm.

I know we had food in the house over the Christmas period. The previous January I had ordered hampers from our milkman, Mr. Orrels. He owned the dairy in Newtown. From the time of William's death, this man kept a kindly eye on us. Eggs would be left on the doorstep along with the milk. He brought sacks of potatoes for us on the pretext that he wanted us to try them out. He carefully reminded me about the payments for the hampers all through those long months. When Christmas arrived, Mr Orrels delivered the hampers. There was plenty of food in the house, at least. I forced myself into the kitchen to make the Christmas meal, aware that my inability to behave normally was hurting the family. I made myself concentrate on cooking so that I could produce the meal. I refused to let myself think about anything else and put every effort into it. I laid the table and put out the food. We all sat around the table and it was only then that I realised I had laid places for everybody. William's seat was empty. Nobody mentioned it as they sat and ate their meal but I saw them glance at the vacant place and I saw their silent tears.

William's birthday was on January 9. It should have been his nineteenth birthday. I began to have acute pains in my body for many hours before the actual day. I awoke in agony and looked at the clock. It was eight minutes past three in the morning. This was exactly the time that he was born, nineteen years ago. That was a difficult day for me. I became disorientated and confused, often forgetting that nineteen years had passed and wondering where my baby was.

In the days leading up to the trial, life with the press at the door had become more difficult. They climbed on the wall and tried to look through the windows, so we had to keep the curtains shut. They pushed notes through the door that told us it was our chance to tell our side of the story and it wouldn't cost us anything. I didn't feel the need to tell them anything. William and Fiona had not *chosen* to be murdered. That *was* the story, there were not two sides. On more than one occasion we had to ask the police to remove journalists and cameramen when they would not stop banging on the door. Nobody had warned us that this would happen. Nobody advised us about how to deal with them. I often wished that we could go somewhere quiet where we would be allowed to grieve in peace.

Perhaps we would be left alone once the trial was over. I looked forward to that day. The trial would provide answers to my questions - I knew that because that is what trials are all about. I would see the face of the killer and hear why he had murdered William and Fiona. It wasn't that I was looking forward to the trial - I was looking forward to getting the trial over with. I believed that once I understood who had killed them and why and how, I would be able to start making sense of it. I would no longer be tormented with questions. I might even be able to start the healing process. That was what I looked forward to.

The trial was listed for 14 January 1997 at Chester Crown Court. I dreaded it and needed it all at the same time. I anticipated that it would be like a painful medical intervention. It would hurt, but things would get better after that. I promised myself that I would be brave.

CHAPTER 6

Prosecution

As we walked towards Chester Crown Court the press ran at us. Cameras were thrust in my face as they jostled with one another to get the best view. I was attending in order to find out why my child was dead. I thought that they should have shown respect. It should have been a quiet and dignified entrance. Instead it felt like the race for bargains on the opening day of the sales.

I was to be a witness and was therefore not allowed to go into the courtroom. Instead, I was introduced to the Witness Service representative, who ushered me into a small room where I could sit and wait. The carpets were stained and the room smelled musty. It was so different from the grand entrance to the building. John Hedges had told us that he had arranged for a room to be available for us during the trial and I presumed that this was it. I could at least have privacy. I waited for a little while but I became more and more anxious, wondering what was happening in the courtroom, how long I would have to wait and what it would be like to give evidence. It wasn't long before I wished that I were with my family. The privacy began to feel like abandonment. I was alone. I might be forgotten. I didn't want to be alone. Then I started to become fearful about entering court and giving evidence. I had no idea what this would involve. Feeling abandoned and afraid, I began to cry.

The door opened and it was Sergeant Price. His eyes quickly scanned the little room and I saw a shadow come across his face.

'Have you been left in here on your own?' he asked and I could tell that he was unhappy about it. He told me that he would be back in just one minute and soon returned to explain that I was no longer required to give evidence. He had organized the seating arrangements in the courtroom and took me in, explaining, as we made our way there, that counsel for prosecution was making his opening submission and that they had just been agreeing some photos and plans of Llandod with the defence so that they could be shown to the jury when needed. I wiped my eyes and composed myself before entering. I was so determined to represent my son in a dignified manner. I knew that I must be quiet and simply sit and listen. This was what I had been waiting to hear for many months. I took a deep breath and went in.

•   •   •

It was a big room, very grand with a high ceiling and pillars, wood panelling on the walls and polished wooden benches. I was seated with Brian, Sue and my mum. On the bench in front of us were Dr and Mrs. Ovis. I could see Andrew Cole. He was in the dock, which was like a wooden pulpit. I could not see his face as I had a side view of him but I noticed that he was wearing a smart, dark green suit with a shirt and tie and that he had his hair combed back into a pony tail. Lord Thomas, counsel for prosecution, was on his feet in front of the judge. In his wig and black gown, he commanded attention as he spoke.

He was talking about Andrew Cole, describing how he had been admitted to the Mid-Wales Hospital in Talgarth in November 1995. His stay in there had overlapped with that of Fiona Ovis by three weeks. Theirs was the first sexual relationship he had ever had and he had been infatuated with her. In April 1996 she made it clear that she did not wish to continue the relationship. She had entered into a relationship with 'Ronnie' Crompton and that was fatal to the both of them. I was surprised to hear William being referred to by his nick-name, Ronnie. It was a name used by his friends, rather than at home where he was always William.

Lord Thomas went on to explain that Andrew Cole was very upset when Fiona had ended their relationship and he went back into hospital as a crisis admission. He had been given a mild sedative and his mental state was assessed. At half past eight in the evening of April 30, Andrew Cole's father had collected him from the hospital. The following day he had seen Fiona with William. He had seen them go to the bungalow and in the early hours of the morning he had killed them. There were no independent eye witnesses. He had gone to the bungalow and heard them making love. He had stuck a microphone through the letterbox of the bungalow, then re-wound the tape and stood at the back door, listening to it. He ran around the house, found a bird table and threw it through the bedroom window. With a boulder he had knocked out the rest of the glass and dived through the window. He had a torch and could see them in bed with it. He had a knife in his possession. It had been with him ever since the Friday when he went into Talgarth Hospital. He stabbed at William, who he described as being violent and in borstal all of his life. William charged at him with a duvet, then William was on the floor, bleeding. Fiona was sitting up in bed and said nothing as Cole stabbed her through the head. He admitted stabbing at their genitals, but said that he was stabbing at random.

There was so much going through my head as I listened to this. I was disgusted to hear William being described as violent. William had never been a fighter, his friends used to tease him that he couldn't fight his way out of a wet paper bag. This didn't worry them or William. William had not been in borstal all his life. He had been in trouble. He had been in custody. He had hated every minute of it, though and had turned his life around rather than go back there again.

I could picture the bungalow. I had been there. The bedroom was small. If anyone had thrown a bird table through the window, it would have landed on the bed. They would have got out of bed and screamed and run out of the bedroom. It would have been chaos. Andrew Cole would not have been able to then smash the rest of the glass out of the window, dive into the bedroom and then turn on his torch to see them in the bed making love. This was nonsense!

Dr. Ovis was the first witness. He was a smart man, around sixty years of age with grey hair. He was dressed in a dark suit with a white shirt and a dark tie. I noticed that his movements were slightly stiff and that dread showed in his progress as he took the witness stand. His face showed strain, his cheeks were slightly hollow and there were shadows beneath his eyes. On the day I lost my son, this man lost his daughter. She was their only daughter. Lord Thomas questioned him and he was required to explain about Fiona's mental health problems, which included sleep disorder, fatigue and depression. I could see that this hurt. I wondered if he felt that the victims were being judged. Fiona's doctor was Dr. Christine Foy, a consultant psychiatrist. In September of 1995, Fiona had overdosed and been discharged three days later. Three days? I wondered if he meant three weeks. Lord Thomas had just said that Andrew Cole had been admitted in November and Fiona's stay in hospital had overlapped by three weeks. This wasn't questioned. Perhaps the pain in his eyes held off such questioning.

But there were questions about Fiona's previous relationships. My heart went out to her father. His head bowed slightly. It was like watching him taking a public whipping. Fiona was not a child. She was twenty-eight years old when she was murdered. It would have been odd if she didn't have previous relationships. Two relationships in particular were discussed. Tristan and Graham had also been mental health patients. Graham had threatened suicide when their relationship ended.

Fiona had mentioned William to her father, but he was only spoken of as a friend, whilst she had referred to William as 'a little additional brother'. I too had thought their relationship was one of friendship. Dr. Ovis said he was introduced to Andrew Cole on 29 November 1995. From January 1996, Cole had been a frequent visitor to their home. Dr. Ovis had once met Fiona and Andrew Cole while they were out shopping in Shrewsbury. They had spent a weekend in the bungalow in April. So, I noted, Andrew Cole had stayed in the bungalow and slept with her in that same bed, upon which he was to brutally murder her.

My glance kept returning to the dock as Dr. Ovis gave evidence. Andrew Cole's head was bowed, not in shame, but because he was busy making notes. Frequently he passed notes to his own counsel and defence advocate.

When he had finished giving evidence, Dr. Ovis returned to his seat. I was so glad that I hadn't been required to go through such an ordeal. I had been through too much already. Giving evidence might have finished me off. I wished that I could reach out to Dr. Ovis and say something comforting but I remained still in my seat.

A social worker, Helen Kiterley, was the second witness. She described how Andrew Cole had come to her on April 26 and told her that Fiona had slept with someone else and was in love with this man. Cole was so upset about this that she made arrangements for him to be re-admitted to the Mid-Wales Hospital in Talgarth.

Cole was very keen to see his doctor, Dr Christine Foy. Dr Foy was the person he most wanted to see in the entire world. He was not able to see Dr Foy on May 1, she was not available and he had agreed to take the first cancellation.

I thought about that date. On May 1, Cole had gone to the bungalow. In the early hours he had killed William and Fiona. This was the first time I wondered if things could have been different. It was not to be the last.

The third witness to take the stand was Dr Hessian. Until May 3 he had been the consultant psychiatrist at Talgarth Hospital, but was now retired. He said he had first met Andrew Cole on November 16 and that Cole had remained in care until January 11. He was discharged then and became an out-patient at the Hazel Centre. This was a support centre for people suffering from problems with their mental health. There was much discussion about Cole's mental condition. They talked about personality disorders and psychotic illness, excessive compulsory disorder and paranoid traits. It was all very complicated but I got the impression that the doctor was saying that Cole had a personality disorder, not a formal psychotic illness. He then went on to describe Cole in glowing terms, as charming and intelligent. He said that Cole had been given a low dose of a psychotic drug when he was admitted in November but it had a reducing effect. This had upset Cole and he hadn't been forced to continue with it. After three weeks there was no evidence of any need for medication.

Dr Hessian said that Cole had met Fiona Ovis at the end of November, 1995. He met her whilst on leave. She visited regularly when Cole moved into his flat. At that time she was unravelling herself from a relationship. There had been an introduction between the families and an intense sexual attachment had developed on Cole's part. Dr Hessian was asked about Cole's discharge and he also referred to Cole's desire to see Dr Foy at the end of April.

The witness was then handed a paper. I noticed a look of outrage register on his face. He appeared shocked that the paper was in court. This paper was a draft that he had written on May 5. He said it was merely an attempt, while events were fresh in his mind, to make a record of contact and dealings with Andrew Cole since birth. How odd, I thought. Wasn't that what medical records were for? Should all the contact and dealings with Andrew Cole not be recorded precisely on formal hospital records?

There was much discussion about Cole's childhood, how he would have nothing to do with his mother, only his grandmother. Eventually he had locked himself inside his flat and would only speak to his mother through the closed door. Social services had attempted to make contact with him, but he still wouldn't open the door. In November he had been physically removed as a Section 135 Mental Health Act admission. During the following three weeks he was seen by Dr Foy. There were eight case conferences and no medication. Cole was unhappy about taking drugs and there was no clinical reason for them.

I suppressed the urge to stand up and start shouting. I wanted to shout out 'Hang on a minute, that doctor has just contradicted himself. He's just said that Andrew Cole didn't take any medication but earlier on he said he gave him a low dose of a psychotic drug. He's reading from notes he made four days after the murders were committed. Where are all the formal records? What's going on?'

I was alert now, listening intently. I sensed something wrong. I had come to court to hear a murderer say why he had killed my son. I had expected him to try and excuse his behaviour in some way. It was his chance to try and explain his actions, to try and say that it wasn't his fault. I was prepared to hear searching questions put to him so that he would be forced to face the facts. I had expected that here, in a court of law, lies would be exposed and the facts would be examined. On the witness stand was a prosecution witness, a doctor, a consultant psychiatrist, no less. I should have been able to sit and listen to him give the court some medical facts about the murderer. Instead, I felt the hairs prickle at the back of my neck. Perhaps there were enemies of justice in this court.

Dr Hessian continued talking about Cole. He described him as quiet, gentle and charming. There was no evidence of a formal psychiatric illness. He was asked if there must have been something wrong with Cole for all this to have happened and he agreed. Then he said something extraordinary. He said that he wanted to read the clinical notes to correct mistakes. What did he mean by mistakes? Why would there be mistakes on clinical notes? These notes were evidence, they should not be interfered with and they should be used during this trial. There were no clinical notes used in evidence. There was only the report that this doctor had written after the murders. Was he withholding them? Why was he allowed to do this?

His evidence went on for some time, during which he again referred to Andrew Cole as a gentle young man. I wished that I could air my views. Three days after a patient has stabbed two people to death, a consultant psychiatrist writes a report in which he describes him as 'a gentle young man.' I wondered how much he knew about the patients in his care.

I went home after the first day of the trial with my mind working busily on all the information that I had heard. It had been a disappointment to me to find out that the trial was going to go on for days. I had imagined that we were going to go in and hear the evidence in one day. I hadn't been warned about the length of the proceedings. I had been expecting to hear something from Andrew Cole. I didn't know how long the trial would go on before he actually spoke. I couldn't stop thinking about him and how he had made notes while each of the witnesses gave evidence.

●　　●　　●

I gave much thought to the evidence I had heard. It was so frustrating to sit quietly and let other people ask questions. Sleep evaded me that night. I drifted into a light doze but constantly awoke. I tried to relax so that I would be refreshed for the next day. I knew I would have to be capable of concentrating. There was so much that I desperately needed to know and there were worrying signs that it might not be as easy to satisfy my need for the truth as I had hoped.

CHAPTER 7

More Questions than Answers

The next morning we made our way into court, hiding our faces from the press who, once again, surged towards us shouting for us to look at the cameras. Someone from the press had been in court and taken notes when I was waiting to give evidence in the little witness room. Brian could not keep the information from me any longer now that the details were in print. William had been stabbed twenty one times and slashed seventeen times, making a total of thirty-eight wounds. He had injuries to his neck, chest, genital area and his jugular vein was severed. Fiona had over twenty stab wounds, eight to her head and neck, twelve to her chest and genital area. She had thirty slash wounds. There were injuries to her hands from defending herself. Her left artery had been severed.

I was determined that this knowledge would not prevent me from listening and concentrating. There would be plenty of time to think about it after the trial. Until it was over, I needed to be stronger than I had ever been before.

We sat in the same places as we had done the day before. The next witness was Dr Christine Foy. This was the doctor who Andrew Cole had been so desperate to see before he murdered Fiona and William. She confirmed her details and said that she had worked at the Mid-Wales Hospital since November, 1995. So, I mentally noted, she was a new member of staff when Andrew Cole was first admitted. She said very little and gave evidence for only a short time. She had been involved with his admittance in November and this had come about through concerns expressed by his mother. He became a voluntary patient some time after that and they had expected to find more wrong with him than they actually did. He was discharged on January 16. I was sensitive to the dates she stated and remembered that Dr. Hessian had said that he had been discharged on January 11. I thought that these inconsistencies and frustrations would have been cleared up if the formal records had been presented.

●　　　●　　　●

Andrew Cole's mother was called to the witness stand. She was a small woman, with gingery-brown hair. She seemed timid. She said that her relationship with her son had broken down when she told him that she was expecting her second child. She said that he would not accept food prepared by her or allow her to wash his clothes. His grandmother had to do those things for him. He had joined the army but had to leave because of a knee injury. After that he spent the next ten years more or less shut away in his flat, which was above their shop. He remained awake all night and slept all day. He didn't go out during the day, except when she took him to driving lessons in Hereford.

When he was forcibly removed from his flat and taken to Talgarth Hospital, he was angry and blamed his mother. After a few weeks he accepted that he was alright in the hospital and stopped blaming her. He was discharged from hospital the first weekend in January 1996 but would still not eat anything that she had touched, so his grandmother visited him every weekend and cooked for him. When he and Fiona visited them in January, Fiona sat at the table and he sat on a separate stool and ate his grandmother's food.

On April 25 he rang his mother and told her that he was very distressed. The following day, Friday, April 26, he rang her from the Hazel Centre to say that he had not been able to see Dr Foy and that he had a better chance of seeing her when he went into hospital. On Wednesday, May 1 he telephoned his mother to say that he felt ill and that he still loved Fiona and wanted her back. Mrs Cole found out about the murders from the Welsh news.

Before leaving the stand she was asked if there was anything that she wanted to say and she answered that she wanted to offer her condolences to the families of the victims. I gave her no sign that I was pacified by what she had said. I wanted the perpetrator to be sorry, not his mother! But I did pause for a moment to think about what an awful shock it must have been to hear of her son's arrest on the news.

I also noted that the first weekend in January was Saturday, January 6 and 7. I wondered when Andrew Cole had really been discharged from hospital. So far, everyone had given a different date. Perhaps Lord Thomas was waiting until the witnesses had all been examined and he would then point out these discrepancies when he summed up the evidence.

A friend of Andrew Cole, Jane Boyes, was the next witness. In November, 1995, she had also been a patient at Talgarth Hospital and had become friends with him. On April 27 he telephoned her to tell her that that he was back there. She went to the hospital to visit him and he told her that Fiona had slept with somebody else. Fiona had said she wanted to be friends with Cole, not his lover. He could not understand this. The following day she went to visit him again. She took her two children with her. She was aware that Fiona telephoned him while they were there to visit. On April 30, Andrew Cole telephoned her to say that he was leaving the hospital because Dr Foy was away.

Catherine Powell, a staff nurse at Llandrindod Wells hospital was called next. On Wednesday, May 1 she was working the night shift that took her through until seven o'clock the following morning. Around twenty past one in the morning of May 2 she noticed someone approach the door. She and Nurse Middleton went to open it. Andrew Cole was there. He was shaking and anxious. He produced a knife and said 'I give this to you in evidence.' She went to 'phone 999 while Nurse Middleton stayed with him. She then went back to reception and Andrew Cole was sitting in a chair waiting for the police to arrive. He said that he had murdered two people. He wanted an ambulance to go to them. He said that they needed help. The police arrived quickly and she handed the knife to them. She and Sister Breeze got a wheelchair and took Andrew Cole to casualty. He was calm as she removed his trousers to find a cut, two inches below his right knee. He said that he had stabbed himself while he was stabbing them. While she was cleaning him up, she noticed that his right hand was clenched into a fist. She unclenched his fist and found hair in it. She put the hair in a bag to give it to the police. She removed his clothing and also gave that to them. Dr Hilsden gave instructions on how to deal with the wounds. When asked if Dr Hilsden had insisted on treatment she said that he had. Throughout this treatment, Andrew Cole talked to them - he was calm, lucid and cooperative. He had cut a tendon in his right hand, which was bandaged up after treatment.

Nurse Gertrude Middleton confirmed much of this when she gave her evidence. There were differences, but people remember things different ways. According to her, it was ten past one when she saw a car driving up to the entrance of the hospital. The doorbell rang continuously and she went with Nurse Powell to answer it. When the door opened, Cole looked calm. He had a rucksack on his back and a knife, which was closed, in his hand. He handed in the knife and a can of fly spray, which he took out of his jacket pocket. She sat him in a chair while her colleague went to the office to call 999. She took off his boot and the sock was covered in blood. He asked her if she knew Fiona, which she did. He said that he had murdered her - he had cut her throat and stabbed her through the heart. She asked him why and he said that it was because he loved her.

A statement was then read to the court. It had been made on May 2 by Sister Breeze. She saw 'Gertie' and 'Kate' go the door. She saw a knife on the desk in the sister's office, covered in blood. She gave gloves to the two nurses and put a pair on herself. As Gertie was trying to take Cole's right boot off, she removed the left boot. When she was attending to his leg, he said that he stabbed a boy but killed Fiona Ovis. He gave the address of the bungalow and told them to get an ambulance. When the police left to go to the address, she and Kate took him down to casualty and removed his trousers. He had a laceration on his right leg, below the knee. There were no visible injuries on his chest and his blood pressure and pulse were normal. They filled in a casualty card and Cole was able to give all the relevant details. Then Dr Hilsden came in and spoke to the police officers.

Cole had talked about the murder. Her statement described how he had heard Fiona and William giggling and talking. He had jumped through the bedroom window. He had got William first in the back of his head and then killed Fiona, got her in the heart and slit her throat. He had gone back to William, stabbed him in the chest and cut his penis off so that he couldn't do it to anyone else's girlfriend. He then drove Fiona's car to hospital. He was calm as he talked to Sister Breeze and they had a normal conversation. He wasn't upset and he didn't cry.

●　　●　　●

I felt my stomach heave and struggled to get my breath. My boy had been sexually mutilated by this man who was sitting in the dock and making notes. There he was, seated in a grand room. He was wearing a smart suit. His hair was combed. He had paper and a pen. His comfort offended me. The fact that there had been much comment about his injuries and his welfare was unacceptable to me at that moment. While nurses had been taking his boots off for him and looking at his injuries and taking his pulse, my son and Fiona had lay where he had left them. After what he had done to them, why should it matter to anyone that he had a cut on his leg?

A statement was read out that had been made by Dr. Hilsden on May 2. In it, he said he was the doctor on call at Llandrindod Wells Hospital. He had returned home at eleven in the evening. At seventeen minutes past one he was called out by Nurse Kate Powell. He went back to the hospital and saw Andrew Cole on the bed. He had blood on his hands, face and right leg. He assessed his injuries generally, no treatment was given and then he was called to another patient. He went back to Andrew Cole and assessed that he was in no immediate danger.

The police officers requested that he attend at the bungalow. Upon arrival he was met by a police officer and asked to establish whether anyone was alive. Lights were on in the kitchen and there was no sign of any struggle. The living room was dimly lit and, again, no sign of a struggle. He saw the naked body of a young male with short fair hair face down on the floor. There was blood around the body but no visible wounds or signs of life. Life was pronounced extinct.

I was taken aback. William had short dark hair. His hair was almost black. The statement described that in the bedroom there was a large amount of blood. The window was smashed. A female wearing a black nightie was on the bed. Her face and hair were bloodstained. There was a gash to her neck, from the ear across the windpipe. There were no signs of life. Life was pronounced extinct.

He confirmed that he did not touch anything whilst on the premises. Back at the hospital he saw Andrew Cole. He had the following injuries: a small laceration on his right ear, a deep laceration on his little finger and grazes on his hands. All these injuries were caused by glass. There was also a two inch laceration on his right leg from a knife wound. He was transferred to Morriston Hospital in Swansea for treatment.

Dr Hilsden said that Andrew Cole had asked him if they 'were both dead' and had replied that they were. Cole then said that he had encountered problems finding the keys to Fiona's car but once he found them he had driven straight to the hospital. Dr Hilsden noted that Cole was not under the influence of drink or drugs. He was quite lucid.

PC Westlake was at court and took the witness stand. He was allowed to refer to notes that he had made at four o'clock in the morning. He said that he had attended Llandod Hospital and noticed a white Vauxhall Cavalier car. He had gone inside and saw Andrew Cole, who told him to get an ambulance. Cole said that he had stabbed two people and they were dead. PC Westlake cautioned him and then went outside to get WPC Buskall, who recorded the conversation between PC Westlake and Andrew Cole. These notes recorded the fact that Andrew Cole understood the caution. Cole said that he had waited and listened, he heard them making love. He had picked up the bird table and smashed the window. He tried to undo the latch of a window that he had already broken. He shone the torch on them. William hid under the duvet. He (Cole) always carried a knife. William charged at him. He stabbed William, who stumbled on the floor and went to the next room. He stabbed him again. He didn't mean to. He went back into the bedroom and stabbed Fiona. He didn't mean to. He looked for the keys, found them, went outside, they were the wrong keys. He went back again. It was an automatic car. He wasn't used to it but he drove to the hospital.

During the cross-examination of PC Westlake, defence counsel asked him if Dr Hilsden was at the hospital or at the bungalow when he spoke to Andrew Cole. In answer, he said that Dr Hilsden was not at the hospital. This did not seem like an answer to me, it seemed like an evasion. I wished that counsel had asked him to clarify the information, but he did not.

WPC Buskall then took the stand and said that the Vauxhall Cavalier still had its headlights on when she arrived at the hospital at one-thirty in the morning. The key was in the ignition and the inside and outside of the car was heavily bloodstained. PC Westlake came back out from inside the hospital and then they both went inside again. They were handed the heavily bloodstained knife. WPC Buskall recorded the conversation between PC Westlake and Andrew Cole in her notebook.

PC Roach was called next. He had been instructed to go the hospital, on prisoner duties, at four thirty in the morning. The prisoner, Andrew Cole, was lying in bed. Cole had asked PC Roach if he knew the victims and when 'it would be in court and if the press would hear about it'. He told PC Roach that Fiona's feelings for William were stronger than her feelings for him. He had listened to them making love. The sounds of them laughing had made him mad. He had smashed a window and used the torch to see his way. PC Roach quoted Cole as saying, 'I drove at sixty miles per hour down to hospital.' Cole then slept for a while.

During another sleepless night and many nights since, I have tried to piece together what happened at the hospital from the arrival of Cole until his departure. Andrew Cole arrived there and handed in a bloodstained knife. He told the nurses that he had stabbed two people. The police quickly arrived and found him sitting in a chair, waiting for them. Nurse Powell gave them the knife. The police spoke to Andrew Cole, cautioned him and then went off to the address that he gave. Sister Breeze and Nurse Powell took Cole down to casualty in a wheelchair. They removed his clothes and cleaned him up. While they were cleaning him up, Nurse Powell noticed that he was clutching his right fist. She opened his fist and took out some hair, which she put in a bag, ready to give to the police. Dr Hilsden arrived and assessed Cole's injuries. He went to see to another patient and then returned to Cole. The police asked him to attend the bungalow, to see if anybody was alive. This suggests that the police officers left the hospital and later returned, by which time Dr Hilsden had arrived.

I think about the two police officers. They arrived at the hospital to be handed a bloodstained knife and to hear that Andrew Cole says that he has stabbed two people. They cautioned him, asked him questions, took notes of that conversation and then they left to go and look at the address he gave them. The knife, the blood and the suspect himself all suggested that Cole really had stabbed two people. So they left him and the knife with 'Gertie', 'Kate' and Sister Breeze. Did they think, even for a second that this murderer might decide to escape? Did they wonder if he might lose control again and decide to stab Kate and Gertie? No, they left him right there in the hospital. They didn't put handcuffs on him and they didn't wait until other officers arrived. They left him in the hospital where the nurses continued to do what they had been trained to do. What they had not been trained to do is to preserve evidence. They cleaned him up. The police officers wandered off, leaving the nurses to clean away the evidence from the murderer.

By the time Dr Hilsden arrived, Cole was already in casualty. The police officers had already left and may have returned. I wondered if that was why PC Westlake avoided answering the question that was put to him in court. He was asked if Dr Hilsden was at the hospital or the bungalow when he, PC Westlake, questioned Andrew Cole. Perhaps he didn't want to say that Dr Hilsden had not yet arrived at the hospital when they were questioning Andrew Cole and that they left the hospital before Dr Hilsden arrived. The fact that Dr. Hilsden took some time to arrive was, however, understandable. As the doctor on call that night, he was probably fast asleep in bed when the telephone call came.

In his statement, Dr Hilsden said that no treatment was given to Cole but Nurse Powell said that Dr Hilsden gave instructions to deal with the wounds; she said that Dr Hilsden insisted on treatment. She had been asked to refer to her statement and read out to the court that Cole had talked to them all through his treatment. She had given details. Cole had cut a tendon in his right hand and this had been bandaged up after treatment. It seems to me most likely that Dr Hilsden really had given the instructions on the treatment of Cole. There are too many details in the statement of Nurse Powell for this to be a slip of the mind on her part. She had referred to her statement while under oath. The statement was made on May 2. This was the same date as the murders. She therefore gave written details about the treatment of Andrew Cole only hours after that treatment had been given.

Why, I asked myself, did Dr Hilsden have Cole transferred to Morriston Hospital in Swansea when he had insisted on treatment being given to Cole by the staff in Llandod? Cole had cut his right hand and it had been bandaged up after treatment. He had a laceration to his right leg, two inches below the knee. Dr Hilsden had seen him and been satisfied that he was in no danger and had gone to the bungalow. When he came back from the bungalow he looked at Cole again and listed his injuries. These were a small laceration on his right ear, a deep laceration on his little finger and grazes on his hands. All these injuries were caused by glass. There was also a two inch laceration on his right leg from a knife wound. Nurse Powell states that Cole had a cut tendon on his right hand. As the only injury on his right hand was a deep laceration on his little finger, it must be the case that Cole had cut a tendon in the little finger of his right hand. Cole was transferred to Morriston Hospital in Swansea for treatment. I couldn't understand why the injuries required this transfer. It appeared that Dr Hilsden went to the bungalow with no particular concerns about Cole's injuries but when he returned from there he felt the need to have Cole transferred. Why the sudden need to get Cole away from Llandod?

One other thing I noticed about the statement made by Dr Hilsden on May 2 is that he states that Cole was not under the influence of drink or drugs. How does he know? To find out that information, he would have to take blood samples and send them away for testing. Then he would have had to wait for the results. He can't know, on that same day, that Cole is not under the influence of any drugs. Possibly Dr Hilsden meant to say that Cole did not appear to be under the influence of drink or drugs. If that is the case, then that is what really ought to have been noted on the statement. Dr Hilsden was not called to give evidence. His statement was read out to the court as part of the case for the prosecution. This indicates that the defence did not wish to challenge any information that was given on his statement. There were things that I wanted to challenge, though. I wished that I could ask him a few questions.

Other possibilities have occurred to me. Statements from the witnesses who were at Llandrindod Hospital that night describe how Cole not only told them that he had killed, but who he killed. He asked them if they knew Fiona. They did. Llandod is a small place. Dr Ovis and Dr Hilsden are both local GPs and based at the same surgery. Did Dr Hilsden go to the hospital from his home, that night? If the nurse telephoned him and told him that Fiona Ovis had been stabbed at the bungalow that had belonged to her grandparents, would he have gone to the hospital first or would he have gone straight round to the bungalow? What else was happening during these hours? What information was not given to the court?

Often during my disturbed nights, I have thought about Andrew Cole, having his wounds treated in hospital whilst, perhaps, William and Fiona lay unattended in the bungalow. I think about the way the case was dealt with. I picture a murderer being left in hospital, being cleaned up before anyone from forensics arrived. I wonder if that is what happened. I wonder about what evidence has never come to light. Whose hair was in Cole's hand? Whose blood was in the car? How did he drive a car with his hand clenched into a fist? I imagined that Cole would have been covered in the blood of his victims after the frenzied stabbing that resulted in so many wounds. William's jugular vein was severed during the attack. There is very little evidence to suggest that he was covered in blood to the extent that this caused a great shock when he arrived at the hospital. The blood on the steering wheel, the car and on his clothes could have come from his own injuries. I think about all the questions that remain unanswered and I wonder what was concealed among the inconsistencies and implausibilities that went unchallenged in the court throughout the trial.

CHAPTER 8

A Killer's Statement

On the third day of the trial, we arrived at court and took up our seats. It was fairly quiet and people were speaking to each other in the more relaxed atmosphere whilst awaiting the arrival of the judge. I saw a police officer who I did not recognise. There was something about him that drew me to him. I had stopped trying to worry about whether or not my behaviour was that of a sane woman and allowed my instincts to guide me. I went over to him and said 'Excuse me, I'd like to shake your hand and thank you for being so kind to my William, even though he was dead.' He obviously knew who I was and shook my hand, warmly. 'That's alright, Wendy. It was the least I could do.' I went back to my seat and Sergeant Price said that Dave Mills had indeed been very kind to William and ensured that, at all times, his body was treated with the utmost respect. I didn't know how I knew that this officer had been looking after my son for me, when I could not have. Perhaps William pointed him out to me. I'd like to think he did. Sergeant Price then went on to tell me how Dave Mills had stayed up all night, typing out Cole's interview and making sure it was perfectly accurate, so that it could go to the Crown Prosecution Service the following morning.

•   •   •

The civilian scenes of crime officer was called as a witness and told the court that he went to the bungalow, and recovered a pedal cycle. He carried out a forensic examination at the scene and also received, from the Home Office pathologists, the objects that had been sent for scientific examination. He was present at the post mortem examinations. There was only one question put to him in cross examination and that was to enquire if he had found two cigarette ends at the scene, which he had.

Detective constable David John, from the Llanelli Scenes of Crime Department took the oath next. He had attended at Llandod hospital and photographed the evidence. He had noted the Vauxhall car on arrival. He took pictures of Andrew Cole, showing his injuries and also of the blood stained clothing that had been removed from Cole - before collecting these items in evidence bags. He examined the contents of Cole's rucksack. These were - gloves, a notebook, a Yorkie bar, a biro, keys, an elasticated rope, a grey flask containing a clear liquid, a purse containing £440 and a Casio micro cassette recorder with a tape inside it. He sent the clear liquid from the flask off for analysis (this being, as confirmed later in the trial, a 'light petroleum distillate').

Lord Thomas for the prosecution asked him if he listened to the tape. He said that he had, at the police station, next day. He could hear nothing on the tape. In cross-examination, he was asked if there was a can of fly spray and he agreed. He also agreed that he found cigarettes, a green lighter and a plastic container, within which were matches, in the right pocket of Andrew Cole's jacket.

Christopher Pitchford, QC, Cole's defence advocate, pointed out that it looked as though there was a tape inside the cassette recorder. He asked DC John if he had handed that tape to anybody else and he replied that he had not, it had been retained in Llandrindod Wells Police Station overnight and then in his possession until he listened to it. He was asked if he had listened to the tape from the very beginning to the end. He had. It was suggested to the witness that pop music was on the very beginning of the tape. He said that there was not.

I remembered discussion about that tape with Sergeant Price when Brian and I first went to Llandod Police Station. There had been something about Meat Loaf playing on it. There were sounds made by William and Fiona - but it was 'not of their dying breaths'.

Statements were then read out to the court – first those of Nicole Johnstone and Martin Morris. They were a couple and stated that they had gone out with Fiona and William on the evening of May 1. They had gone in their car and Fiona and William had gone in Fiona's car. They had driven over to the Elan Valley and gone for a walk before driving back to Llandod. At eleven o'clock that night, Fiona and William had left for the bungalow.

The next statement was that of Catherine Taylor who was a friend of Cole. Cole had to gone to her house on May 1 to see her. He cried and told her how upset he was that Fiona and he had split up and how Fiona had found someone else. He left there at eight-thirty in the evening. Then DC David Mills gave evidence that he had formally arrested and cautioned Andrew Cole on Tuesday May 7 at eight-forty-five in the evening and started to interview him.

I thought about the times involved. Andrew Cole arrived at Llandrindod Wells Hospital at around one-ten in the morning of May 2 and said that he had killed two people. He wasn't formally arrested and cautioned until May 7 at eight-forty-five in the evening. The delay bothered me.

DC Mill's first interview was recorded on tape. Cole was interviewed for just nine minutes before the interview was concluded. The transcript was read to the court. Cole said that he left Catherine Taylor's home at six-thirty in the evening. She was pleased to see him and he told her what had happened between Fiona and William. He was crying. Between nine-thirty and ten in the evening he went to see if Fiona's car was at her friend's house. He then went home and listened to tapes that he and Fiona had listened to together. He didn't want to continue with the interview. He wanted time to think.

He had just had nearly a whole week to think about it. Now he demanded more time to think, and got it. I couldn't help but reflect that he hadn't given William and Fiona any time to think about things or given them any choices.

There was a second interview, conducted the following day. This time Cole told his garbled story. He said that he gone round to see his friend, Cath. He cycled home and saw Fiona's car outside Nicole's. He went home, then went walking and then went back to his flat. Later, he went out walking again and saw Fiona's car go past. He went back to his flat and changed, packed his rucksack and cycled around Llandod. He then dumped his bike and walked to the bungalow. He had never seen William - who he always referred to as 'Ronnie' - and wanted to see him. He saw a light on, he listened, he sat at the back of the house and had a cigarette. He heard music in the bedroom, he squatted outside the front door, listening.

He stuck a microphone through the letterbox and then sat by the garage again. He played the tape and heard music and moans and groans. He turned it off. He didn't want anybody to hear him. He left the rucksack by the garage. He ran round the front of the house, threw something at the window and smashed it. He picked up a bird table and smashed the window - and looked in with a torch. He had a knife with him that he had been carrying since Friday. He could see them in bed. He just walked towards them. He stabbed William who, he said, was a violent man and had been in borstal all his life. William dived at him. Cole walked back through the door and stabbed William until he did not come at him any more.

Fiona sat on the bed. William let out a roar before Cole went in and then charged at him. Cole was stabbing Fiona in the head. She said nothing.

Cole picked up the keys and walked to the car but they were the wrong keys. He got another set of keys and started the car and picked up the rucksack. He reversed the car and went to the hospital. The steering wheel was wet with his blood and the knife was in his hand. He told the nurses to get an ambulance. They sat him down and took his boots off. The police came and he gave them directions to the bungalow.

He then went on to describe the days before the murder, how Fiona had ended the relationship and how upset he was. He said that he had left a message for Dr Foy to see him on the Friday before the murders, but she was unavailable. He went to his social worker, Helen Kitely, and told her that he needed to see Dr Foy. Helen Kitely arranged for him to be re-admitted to Talgarth Hospital. He then cycled up to the home of Dr and Mrs. Ovis but there was nobody home. He packed his bag, ready for hospital and then went to the college. Fiona was eating her lunch. He told her that he would see her outside. He told Fiona that he was going back to Talgarth. He then went to Talgarth by taxi. He phoned Fiona from hospital. At eleven-thirty in the evening he phoned her again but she was not there, so he spoke to her father, telling him that he was back in Talgarth and gave him the number he was ringing from. He telephoned Fiona again the next day.

Cole's father came to pick him up from the hospital on Tuesday, April 30 and he arrived back in Llandod at 9.15 that evening. He phoned Jane. He went to see if Fiona's car was outside Martin and Nicky's. He saw Fiona walking down the road at eleven-thirty. He went back to the flat. He went to see Cath and told her that he had been in hospital.

He said that the stuff in his rucksack was what was usually in there. He cycled to the lake in Llandod and sat there for a while on the Wednesday night. The last time he looked at his watch and it was one-sixteen in the morning of May 2. He put the bike in an alleyway and walked to the bungalow. He had fly spray with him to use in self defence, if William was violent. He first realised that William was there when he heard them making love and he flipped.

He was asked to describe what happened and said that he walked around the house, got a bird table and smashed the window. He also smashed the window with a torch. He tried to get in through the door and smashed that, too. He tried to open the door but could not get in that way. He sat outside the house, drinking from his bottle of water and smoking cigarettes and listening to a tape for about half an hour.

He said that he didn't plan it, it 'just happened'. The window at the back was smashed first. They were screaming and shouting. They were shocked. When he put the torch in, he saw them in bed. He just went in. He just wanted to get in there. It happened in minutes. He didn't take the rucksack in. The knife was in his pocket. He went head first through the window. The bed was directly in front of the window. They both sat up in bed. There was no light on. He put the light switch on and walked up to them. He didn't know when the knife came out. He didn't know what was happening, he was just stabbing William. They had the duvet over them and he didn't know who he was stabbing. He had no idea how many stabs. Until William charged at him, in a rug, he couldn't see any injuries. He had to stop William. He hit him with a torch. He didn't know which torch. He only knew he had it at the window. Nobody said anything. William was moving to the other room, on the floor. He continued stabbing William whilst he was on the floor. He didn't know why.

He was asked where in the body he was stabbing. He said he was stabbing on the genitals but he didn't know why. William didn't try to get to the phone or the front door. He went back to the main bedroom. Fiona was sat on the bed, naked. There was no bleeding, he never saw any, but he wasn't looking. He didn't know what he had done to William. He was sure Fiona was naked. He stabbed her, she didn't try to defend herself or stop him. She didn't say anything. He was only there a few seconds. He didn't say anything. He had no idea how many times she was stabbed. He stabbed Fiona on her genitals; he was just stabbing at random.

Cole was asked when he realised they were dead. He said that it was when he was walking around the house, when he was going to the car, when he got the wrong keys. When he was asked about the amount of time he spent outside the bungalow he said that he was looking through the windows, he sat around drinking and smoking and he went to the letterbox last.

He said that he was carrying the knife for the same reason that he always carried it, he was considering suicide. He was also considering suicide by setting fire to himself.

It was put to Cole that there was a chair in the bedroom doorway. He said that he didn't put it there. He thought that he got the car keys from the sitting room and he also remembered taking the back door keys and letting himself out. Fiona, he was told, had withdrawn £600 and there was only £100 left. He said that it was nothing to do with him, maybe it was William. He did have money in his rucksack but £255.00 was Christmas and birthday money. He also had £128 in packets given to him at the Post Office. It was, he insisted, definitely all his money. He didn't take any money from the house. He would have left finger prints on it. He drove her car, a white Vauxhall.

Cole was asked when he last made love to Fiona. He couldn't remember when they last made love but the time before that she said he was brilliant. He was asked if that was an ego boost and agreed that it was. The fly spray, he explained, came from a cupboard at home and he had taken it with him to use like CS gas, in case he bumped into William and he was violent. When a query about backpacking was put to him, he explained that he collected stuff. He would go out more often if it wasn't for his past condition. In 1992, he had gone to Ireland and in 1990 he went to St. Ives. He had also been out 'a few times' in Llandod. This was the end of defence counsel's questions and Cole was asked if there was anything else that he wished to say. He said he had nothing to say and his injuries made him tired. This concluded the interview.

During cross-examination, DC Mills was asked to read out two cards, from Fiona, which had been recovered from Cole's flat. He was also asked to read out a card that had been received at the house of Dr Ovis after the death of Fiona. It had been posted on May 1 and read 'Fiona, you will always be special to me, I love you. Andrew'

The reason for the delay before Cole was interviewed was explained by DC Dave Mills as being because Andrew Cole was in Morriston receiving major surgery on his arm and leg. DC Mills also confirmed that Dr Tegwyn Williams was present and acted as an appropriate adult during the interview. Dr Williams had suspended the first interview that started on May 7 and as a result further questioning was suspended until May 8.

DC Mills was then asked to confirm that he had listened to a tape recording, taken out of the cassette in Andrew Cole's rucksack. He confirmed that this was the case and that the music at the beginning of the tape was that of Meat Loaf. He left the witness stand and the court adjourned for lunch. I spoke to him as we walked from the room. I said that Cole was accusing William of stealing the money and I was furious about it. In Cole's interview, he lied that William was violent and everyone had heard Dave read out the transcript. I wasn't going to allow them to be persuaded that William had stolen Fiona's money, either. I told Dave that if Cole had the money in his possession when he was re-admitted to Talgarth, as he said, then that fact would have been recorded by the staff when Cole arrived at the hospital. Dave raised his eyebrows and smiled, 'You're right, Wendy, they would. I'll get on to that right now.' He went off to sort it out and had the information faxed through before lunch was over. Cole did not have that money with him when he was re-admitted into Talgarth, he had less than seventy pounds with him. I pointed out to Dave that Cole had claimed that the money had been given to him, some was his Christmas money and some was his birthday money. He had murdered William and Fiona in May, more than four months after Christmas. His date of birth had also been mentioned. He was born in June.

●　　　●　　　●

After lunch, Dave Mills continued giving evidence and was able to inform the court that Andrew Cole did not have £400 in his possession when he was re-admitted to Talgarth. Dave Mills really did do a good job of looking after William and making sure that he was treated with respect. He really was very kind to my boy, even though he was dead. I thought more about my urge to approach this man, when I first saw him in court. Whether it was my instincts or my William that had pointed him out, it was accurate information. He told the truth when he gave evidence. He had heard music on the tape and did not lie to support his colleague. He listened to me. He acted upon my suggestion and spent his lunch break following up the possibility that Talgarth would have the information on record. He ensured that the information arrived in court without delay. He did not allow Cole to imply that William had taken Fiona's money. Cole had caused so many injuries to my son. The implication that William had stolen money from Fiona was another injury that Cole tried to inflict upon my dead son but, with the help of this man, I had at last been able to protect him.

CHAPTER 9

Photo of a Murdered Son

I went to my seat again after the lunch break. There was some discussion about photographs and then the evidence of the pathologist was read out. Dr Stephen Leadbeater had attended the bungalow at ten in the morning on May 2. In the rear bedroom was a naked body of a man lying on his front. His head was in the bedroom, with the legs and torso extending into another small hallway. Inside the bedroom there was the body of a female. Both bodies were removed to the mortuary at Hereford Hospital where the identifications took place.

Lord Thomas, the prosecutor, reached forward and picked up a photograph to show around the court. As he spoke, his hand moved and I was suddenly confronted with a large photograph. In front of my eyes was the face of my son, lifeless, bloodied and with a raw, gaping hole taking up the left side of his neck. I felt a noise start to rise from the pit of my stomach. I knew that I must be silent. I must not allow myself to release this noise in the courtroom. I clasped my hand over my mouth and rose from my seat. I had to get out. I had to leave the room before this noise forced its way from my body. I moved to the door and as I struggled to get there I passed close to the dock. Our eyes met. With the image of my butchered son burning into my head, they met with those of his killer. I registered the terror in his eyes, or was it the reflection of the terror in my own? I didn't know. I stumbled from the room and made my way to the little room where I had waited to give evidence. I opened the door and unfriendly faces were turned on me. I tried to mutter an apology and reeled back, this time making my way to the entrance. I stepped into the outside world where the press were ready to snap and click with their shiny cameras. I looked at them and held up my hand, signalling a 'NO'. Whatever they saw in front of them had the desired effect. They actually lowered their lenses - and their eyes. I moved to a corner, hid my face against the wall and let the noise force its way through my throat. I would describe it as a howl. I banged my head against the wall in an effort to shatter the image of that photograph of William.

I hated the fact that I had been forced to go outside, in public view, in order to release my agony. Then another image came into my head. It was of the faces that had turned towards me when I tried to enter the witness room. They had turned to me with expressions of surprise, the sort of expression you would have on your face if you were intruded upon. I had intruded upon their privacy. One of those faces had belonged to a small woman with gingery-brown hair. I had seen her before. I had seen her giving evidence. She was Mrs. Cole. She was with an elderly woman, a man and a girl. The family of the murderer had been seated in privacy in the witness room while I had to face the world with my naked pain. Then my mum was suddenly beside me. She put her arms around me for comfort. She told me that I had upset Andrew Cole. As I left the room, he had begun to howl and was taken down to the cells.

We took a break. I wasn't fit to return to the courtroom straight away. By the time we did return to our seats, Cole was giving evidence. It was only later that I learnt that the jury had to be sent out when Cole was removed from court. There was a question over whether or not he was fit to give evidence. His defence advocate, Christopher Pitchford QC, had been to see him in the cells and Dr Foy had then been asked to go down and see him in order to assess his fitness to go into the witness box. Evidently he had recovered himself, because he was now in the middle of his testimony.

•　　•　　•

Cole, under the guidance of Christopher Pitchford, described his feelings for Fiona. He could not accept her desire to end her relationship with him. He understood Fiona to be unsure of whether or not she wished to end it. He kept telephoning her and going to see her to discuss this. He said that he went to the lake with her the day before he was re-admitted to Talgarth Hospital. They had sat holding hands while she explained her feelings. Cole then persuaded her to take him to the bungalow, because he had never been inside it. He went into the bedroom and looked at the bed. They discussed the fact that she and William had made love in that bed. Later, they went back to Cole's flat because his father had arranged to bring a fridge around for him. After his father had left, Fiona said that she had to go home, as she had some college work to do but he went and sat in her car with her and continued the conversation.

He went to The Hazels and wrote a letter to Dr Foy. He needed to see her urgently because of what Fiona had done.

Cole's actions, during the six days before he committed the murders, were discussed. It was clear that he was constantly visiting Fiona, telephoning her, cycling around or walking around places where she might be. When he was not doing that, he was talking to other people about her and about how she had entered into a relationship with William. When he was asked if he had gone to see Helen Kitely on Wednesday, May 1, he gave no answer.

He described the murders. He said that he had gone out on his bike that evening, with his rucksack. He pushed the bike into an alley and walked to the bungalow because he wanted to speak to Fiona. There were lights on in the living-room. The curtains were drawn. He could hear loud music. He wandered around outside the bungalow, listening. He put a microphone through the letterbox and taped the sounds. He listened to the recording using headphones.

When he decided that he could hear them making love, he lost control. He smashed a window and then shone the torch through the window. He saw William and Fiona in bed. He ran around the side of the house and smashed the door. He tried to get in. He then dived, head-first through the window.

He had a torch and a knife. He stood on the bed and knelt down, stabbing William. William charged at him, so he stabbed him. William then turned to go out. Fiona was in bed, sitting up. He walked into the bedroom and stabbed her. He continued stabbing her, whilst staring at the wall. He said that he walked out of the bedroom and in the living-room it began to dawn on him what he had done. He got the back door key and reached the car. They were the wrong keys, so he walked back into the house and picked up the right keys from off the dressing table and walked out of the house. He put his rucksack in the car, reversed it and got to hospital.

During his cross-examination, Lord Thomas asked about his earlier reaction to being shown the photos. Cole said that it was seeing the extent of the injuries, on the photos, that had upset him. In answer to one question he confirmed that he had walked back into the house when he realised that he had taken the wrong keys. He walked back into the bedroom, took the car keys from the dressing table and then walked back out through the living room and the kitchen. He remembered sexually mutilating William, but claimed he did not know why he had done it. He could not remember sexually mutilating Fiona and could not remember any of the comments he made to staff at the hospital in Llandrindod Wells.

Lord Thomas then asked about the relationship between him and Fiona. Cole answered that Fiona still loved him. When it was put to him that she only wanted to be friends with him, he was very clear in his answer. 'I don't believe that.' A transcript of a telephone call between him and Fiona was then produced. One copy was handed to Cole and Lord Thomas read the transcript out loud. The outrage registered on Cole's face. This call had been made when he was in Talgarth, the Monday before he killed them. The transcript revealed that Fiona had told him that he was a nice person but that she could not see both of them. Cole asked her why she didn't see William as a friend and stay with him, Cole. She replied that she had to consider her own feelings. She didn't want to get back with him. Cole said that she might change her mind. He asked her how long it would be before she tired of William. She said that she might never tire of him. She didn't hate Cole, she loved him, but she loved him as a friend. Lord Thomas asked Cole if Fiona wanted to be friends or lovers. Cole replied that she still loved him. He refused to accept that she did not still love him in the same way at the time of the call. He stared at the transcript. His head moved from side to side. He snapped monosyllabic answers. His fury was obvious and it was some time before he calmed down.

Throughout that cross-examination, Cole maintained that he had no intention of harming William and Fiona when he went to the bungalow. That was it! This was the evidence that was to be accepted by the court. Cole's sister Lisa was the next witness. I recognised her from the witness room even before she was asked to confirm her name. I took in very little of it. I absorbed enough to understand that Cole would not touch anything that his mother had touched. He hid when his sister's friends came around. His grandmother did his washing. He had not worked for years. He did not apply for work and he did not claim benefits. His parents gave him money and his grandmother gave him money.

I wanted to know what had happened to my son. I had gone through all this and I was not even near the truth. Cole's version of events was preposterous. Was I to accept that neither William nor Fiona could hear the sound of him going around the bungalow breaking windows and the door? He could not possibly have broken the bedroom window and then shone a torch into the bedroom and seen them making love. It was a tiny room. What had happened in the bungalow that night? I wanted to know. I wanted the truth. I felt that it was ridiculous that blatant lies were being accepted in court. I needed to hear what had happened to my son. Cole had taken my son from me and he was keeping information from me. He should not have been able to do that. William is my son. His death should not be allowed to remain his killer's secret.

•　　•　　•

I went home that evening to yet another night of wakefulness and lay in bed having an internal conversation. I tried, but failed to quieten my mind. I wanted to sleep. I would have welcomed oblivion, even just for a few hours. It was not to be. I thought about court, Cole, William, Fiona, the legal representatives, the witnesses, everybody, alive or dead, who was there in court. I had started to realise who was whom in the court room. I now recognised the family of the accused. I recognised those who were attending from the two hospitals involved. This knowledge was adding to my discomfort. I felt like an outsider in the court. The mother, father, sister and grandmother of Andrew Cole mixed with others in the court so much better than we were able to. They seemed to know all the medical staff with whom the court was peopled.

The nurses from Llandod who had come to give evidence were supported by managers from the hospital. These managers were also supporting the staff from the Mid-Wales Hospital in nearby Talgarth. Fiona's family knew them all well and they all talked together during break times and before the proceedings got underway. They were a tight knit group, either from Llandod or health staff or both. We were outsiders. We were from Newtown and did not have connections with health providers. The exclusion and lack of support made me feel as if I was being disregarded. These people were supporting each other. I was uncomfortable with the extent of the inclusion and support that was being extended to the Cole family. Intellectually, I understood that they were not guilty and should not be blamed. Emotionally, I could not accept things. As outsiders, we had taken the place that I imagined would have been reserved for the family of the accused. I therefore felt that William had somehow taken the place of the accused. William was being judged and we were abandoned.

There was nobody to support me. John Hedges did not stay with us throughout the trial. He told us that a paedophile was on trial and he wanted to see how the case was progressing. I presume that was where he was during those tortuous hours. Obviously we could not supply enough entertainment for him. It was probably too much, I thought, to expect from the man who was representing Victim Support. Why, I wondered, would he bother sitting with the family of a murder victim during the trial of the murderer, when he could find so much more titillating entertainment in the courtroom next door? Fair enough, it was his job and he was being paid to do it but he was never going to let a little thing like William's murder impose upon him, I thought to myself.

Brian was a good stepfather and I had never doubted his love for William but I felt that he could not understand the pain that I suffered. My sister attended court every day, as did my mother. The problem was that they were all traumatised. Brian, Sue and my mother were all suffering the torment of having lost a loved one to a dreadful crime. They suffered during the trial. They heard the descriptions of the injuries that had been inflicted upon William. They saw the photographs. That pain and suffering rendered them incapable of giving support. Any idea that we would be able to support each other was akin to walking into an intensive care unit, withdrawing all the medical staff and telling the patients to look after each other.

•　　•　　•

My sense of isolation, abandonment and grief looked for something or someone, to focus on. That night it was Cole. I hated him. I got the impression that he had stalked Fiona. From the moment she told him that she wanted to end the relationship until the moment he killed her, he never left her alone. He was either following her, discussing the situation with her, talking to her on the telephone or dramatically getting himself re-admitted to a psychiatric unit and going to announce this fact to her. When he wasn't doing that, he was talking to other people about the fact that she had ended the relationship. How many people had he told? I tried to count them up. Dr Ovis, two friends of his, Jane and Cath, his mother, his social worker, Helen Kitely and all the staff in Talgarth. He had then killed her and gone to Llandod hospital, where he had given her name to everybody he had spoken to and announced that he had killed her.

Everyone had been so nice to him. Fiona had tried to be gentle when she ended the relationship. She had not deceived him or ignored him. She had been honest and patient. He had been given his wish and allowed back into Talgarth. He had been allowed to leave when he wanted to. The staff at Llandod hospital had patched him up. The doctor had transferred him to Swansea and nobody had let those nasty policemen anywhere near him for six days because they were going to be really horrid to him and charge him with murder. I hadn't been allowed in to court to see him for the plea and directions hearing, because he wouldn't go into the room if I was there. People were attending court to say how nice he was, how gentle and charming.

I got out of bed. I went downstairs and made a cup of tea. I lit a cigarette. It was four in the morning and I tried to be very quiet so as not to wake up the rest of the household. I was furious. I wanted to scream and rage and smash everything up. I wanted to run to wherever this man was being held and scream 'Let me in! Let me at him! I'm sick of all this nonsense! He killed my boy and now I'm going to rip his head off!'

CHAPTER 10

Take Him Down

The next morning I was back in my seat in Chester Crown Court once again. Dr. Tegwyn Williams, consultant forensic psychiatrist in South Wales, was called to give evidence. He wasn't a particularly tall man - he didn't appear especially charismatic. His dark hair was a little too long and reached below his collar. There was, however, something about his manner. He owned the space he occupied. He was confident. He was, I could tell, someone who was used to making decisions. He was someone who was impressed with himself. I prepared to be unimpressed, and was not disappointed.

Dr. Williams was a witness for the defence and, in answer to questions being asked of him, gave information that caused me to take careful notice of what he had to say. He had been contacted on the day following the incident by Drs Hessian and Foy. They had raised concerns about Cole's state of mind. He had gone to Talgarth to see them. He then assessed Cole at Morriston on May 7. Cole was in Morriston because he had an operation on his hand and leg. Dr. Williams had serious concerns about Cole, who did not have suicidal feelings but then said he couldn't face the trial. He alerted the nurses to bear this in mind. Andrew Cole then took an overdose but was discovered by the police.

This doctor had been present when Cole was interviewed by the police on both May 7 and 8. When asked about the first interview, his answer was, 'I told officers it would be better to start on May 8. The police were getting nowhere, it was better to call a halt and start again the next day.'

I was astounded! I needed to listen to those words again. I replayed them, inside my head. 'The police were getting nowhere...' That interview on May 7 lasted nine minutes. A man, by his own admission, butchers two people. He is charged and interviewed by the police, who have waited almost six days to interview him. Then that interview is stopped by a doctor because they are getting nowhere. This man came over to me as bordering on arrogant. He did not even allow them ten minutes to get anywhere. Where did he get all that power from? How long did he need before he 'got anywhere' when he was talking to people? I wondered how far he would have got after nine minutes and what he would have said if someone had told him that he had to stop and leave it until the next day because he was obviously not getting anywhere.

What else had he just said? Andrew Cole had gone to Morriston because he had an operation on his hand and leg? Andrew Cole took an overdose in Morriston? How was that, then? I needed to think about that, too. Andrew Cole had a deep cut on the little finger of his right hand. The wound was so deep that the tendon had been cut. He also had a two inch cut just below the knee of his right leg. A severed tendon requires special stitches to fasten the two ends together. The wound is then stitched up in the normal way. If I had gone to hospital for that treatment, I would have been home the next day. I would have had to have a splint on my finger for weeks, so that the tendon had time to heal, but I would have been sent home. There was no explanation on offer for the six days that Cole spent in Morriston hospital. The shortage of hospital beds was often an issue that was mentioned in the press. They obviously made a special exception for murderers.

While he was in hospital, recovering from this operation, Andrew Cole managed to take an overdose. How? Where were the tablets? Tablets would not have been left beside his bed. Dr Williams had just said that the nurses were alerted to Cole's suicidal state of mind and, whatever, I had never had tablets left beside my bed when I was in hospital. Cole must have been wandering about. This operation obviously did not leave him confined to his bed. His leg could not be too badly damaged to prevent him from getting up and walking about. Did he not have a guard with him? I would have thought that he would be guarded day and night whilst he was in hospital, in case he tried to escape. Obviously that was not the case. He must have been at liberty to wander about the hospital.

I replayed back even further, to the first startling piece of evidence uttered by Dr Williams. Drs Hessian and Foy had contacted him the day following the incident with concerns as to Andrew Cole's state of mind. The incident he referred to was, I presumed, that little incident when Cole stabbed Fiona and William to death. Drs Hessian and Foy reacted to the news that one of their patients had murdered two people by calling in a forensic psychiatrist because they were worried about his state of mind. Well, Cole wasn't their responsibility any more, was he? He was hardly going to be taken back to Talgarth for them to deal with. Once he had committed his crimes he was the responsibility of the Criminal Justice System. What they were possibly more concerned about were consequences. Their reaction was to call in a forensic psychiatrist. I wondered in what way this would benefit them. Perhaps they were taking advice. They must have realised that they would be required to give evidence. I wondered what advice they had been given. I wondered if it was acceptable that the witnesses had colluded. I was beginning to feel a deep mistrust of doctors. There were too many of them interfering in this business.

Dr. Williams went on to explain that Andrew Cole had a severe personality disorder. He said that Cole did not understand feelings for others and had difficulty recognising his own feelings. This was something over which he had no control. He physically and emotionally avoided his feelings. This could be demonstrated by the fact that Cole had locked himself away for ten years. When Fiona ended the relationship with Cole, he became catastrophically distressed and prepared for suicide. He then went to the bungalow and was confronted with the fact that she and William were in bed together. No longer able to deny that she was having an affair, he was unable to cope and the incident was a direct consequence over which, at the time, he had no voluntary control.

By the time his examination-in-chief was over, I was tight-lipped and furious. Fiona had spent days and days telling Cole that their relationship was over. It would hardly have come as a surprise when he went to the bungalow. Fiona was not having an affair - she had entered into a new relationship.

Cole had not exactly locked himself away for ten years. He had admitted that in 1990 he had gone to St. Ives and in 1992 he had gone to Ireland. People do not generally take holidays from mental illness. His mother also said that he didn't go out during the day, not that he didn't go out. I imagined him sneaking about at night. She took him to Hereford for driving lessons, too. Why would he bother having driving lessons if he couldn't cope with going out?

This doctor, I felt, was cherry-picking the facts. He had also referred to the double murder as an incident on two occasions. I did not find this an appropriate description.

Lord Thomas challenged Dr Williams. He suggested that the doctor had accepted the patient's version of events, which the doctor denied. He questioned the diagnosis. He asked if the personality disorder was something that Cole was born with. Dr Williams' answer included the information that when Cole visited his parents with Fiona, it was at the request of Fiona and Dr Foy. I was interested by that piece of information - it seemed that Dr Foy had directly encouraged the relationship between her patients.

When asked about Cole's action of going out with the wrong keys and going back in again, Dr Williams described this as goal-directed control behaviour. He was challenged about his claim that Cole did not understand feelings and avoided them, by referring to his behaviour on the witness stand, when he began howling. Dr Williams said that it was only when faced with the graphic description that the final seriousness stuck home. He was finally cornered into admitting that Cole did not have a specific personality disorder, but went on to explain that there is a checklist and you must have a certain amount of criteria. Cole fulfilled one or two of many different criteria. This did not mean that he did not have a severe personality disorder. It just meant that it was not one of the well-recognised personality disorders.

Finally he was asked if the trigger for the murders was jealousy. This seemed to fluster him. He said 'No' and then 'Yes', commenting that because Cole saw Fiona and William having sex, it may have been but that, because of Cole's lack of understanding, he was not convinced.

I came to the conclusion that Dr. Williams was describing Cole as 'a bit odd'. He had nothing that anybody had ever diagnosed. I wondered how my personality would look if it was ever studied and little ticks were put in boxes. I wondered how anybody would be diagnosed or described by such methods. I was sure that a lot of us would get the 'a bit odd' mark at the end of the test. I wondered what was considered normal by these people. We are all very different. How does anybody decide who is normal?

The next witness was Dr. Robert Hale, who was a consultant psychotherapist. He had first heard of Andrew Cole before the killings, at a seminar, when Dr Foy had talked about him. That started another alarm bell ringing. If Andrew Cole was the easy patient he had been described as, why had she discussed him at a seminar?

This doctor did not agree with the previous one. Dr Hale decided that Cole's personality disorder was 'obsessional' and 'paranoid'. He also stated that Cole had gone to the bungalow to commit suicide and had suffered from 'acute adjustment disorder' when he got there. Lord Thomas pointed out that acute adjustment disorder was a state of emotional distress that can occur in anyone when major events happen, causing them to become jealous, suspicious, angry or violent. The reply was that the personality disorder was an enduring state of mind, whereas acute adjustment disorder is an isolated incident. He maintained that Cole had an abnormal mind.

The final two witnesses were independent doctors, called by the prosecution to deal with issues that had been raised during the trial. Dr Boyd was a consultant forensic psychiatrist, who had given evidence in over thirty murder trials and Dr Jones was also a consultant forensic psychiatrist. They did not agree with Dr Williams. Each told the court that they believed that Cole had acted out of normal jealousy.

Lord Thomas and Christopher Pitchford each summed up their own side of the argument and then the judge summed up the case. He explained to the jury that Cole had admitted the unlawful killings and it was their job to decide whether he was guilty of murder or manslaughter. He told them that Cole had cut their throats, gone for their hearts and deliberately mutilated their genitals. He asked them if this indicated a frenzied attack or a deliberate killing. Then he added, 'Look at the wounds in the backs of Ronnie and Fiona.'

He briefly summed up the evidence of each of the witnesses, and then he adjourned the court for the day. The jury were to consider their verdict on the following day.

• • •

I went home and began my long wait for the verdict. I waited all day and all night. I went to bed and got up and went to bed again. I sat, I walked, I went to bed and I got up for a cup of tea. Dawn came and I prepared myself for court. We went to court and waited until the jury went out to deliberate. I waited in court. I went outside for a cigarette. I sat on my seat in court and then went outside again. I walked, I smoked, I sat and I got up. An hour had passed. I repeated this process hour after hour, smoking, sitting, walking, looking at the time and waiting again.

Eventually the judge accepted that the jury could not reach a unanimous decision and he instructed them that he would accept a majority decision. Eventually they gave that majority verdict to the judge. Cole looked over to where Dr Foy was sitting, a look of horrified shock upon his face. He was addressed by the judge.

'Andrew Douglas Cole, you have been found guilty of the murders of Fiona Ovis and William Crompton. There is only one sentence I can pass and that is of life imprisonment for each count of murder, to run concurrently. I recommend that your medical records follow you wherever you go. Take him down.'[1]

---

1 At the time of this case the life sentence tariff – the minimum time to be served before the offender could be considered for release by the Parole Board – was, in the case of murder, set by the Home Secretary. It is now set by the sentencing judge in accordance with legislation and guidelines issued by the Sentencing Guidelines Council.

CHAPTER 11

Let Battle Commence

At home I waited for a flood of relief to wash over me. It never came. I waited to feel a reduction in the pain that accompanied my every heartbeat, my every breath, but the pain continued unabated. I found no relief, not even for a moment, nothing could distract me from my torment. Food remained tasteless, sleep offered nothing but disturbing dreams that were little different from my waking thoughts and alcohol just made me weep. There was no past, there was no future. Even day and night blurred together, becoming one long, grey half-light. I was lost, wandering in a featureless landscape that stretched out all around me with no hope of escape.

I tried to focus on the source of the pain. Yes, there was grief, a terrible grief. I had lost my son and all that I had invested in him was gone. From the first stretching of my girth as he grew and stirred inside me, through the anxieties of nurture to the fears and doubts of releasing him into the world as an independent soul, all this was lost. I had pushed food into his tiny open mouth, hoping that it would make him strong. I had bitten on my lower lip as he was inoculated against a host of ills, hoping it was protection from an invisible world of deadly viruses. I had left him with strangers on his first day of school and wept all the way home, bereft and anxious for him. It had taken courage to let him take his first independent ride on a bike, cycling out of my sight. I had applauded as he learnt to talk, to read, to write, to sing, to find out whom he was and what he could do. We had battled with each other as he grew strong and tested the boundaries of his world. I had been there to offer comfort and security when he made mistakes. All that worry, all those fears, all those joys, all gone.

I felt the loss of him as a physical pain. I knew what part of me had been torn out - it was an internal hole that started just under my ribcage and extended all the way down to my womb. The gaping wound would always stay open. I yearned to put my arms around him and tell him that I would make it better. I longed to see his face, to hear his voice. I knew that I would never be able to, not tomorrow or tomorrow or the tomorrow after that.

Beyond my grief I could see Marc and Christopher and Wendy-Lou. I knew that they needed me and that they could see me and speak to me and touch me but that I was dead. I knew that they were hurting and I fought to get back to them. I wanted to wake the corpse that was their mother and tell them that I was, 'Sorry, so sorry'.

I identified the grief for my dead son and knew that I would slowly learn to live with this pain. I knew that I would learn a different way to abide, to take account of this disability. I recognised that there was other pain that was halting this progress. I listened, to try and hear an echo that would tell me what it was. I fumbled, like the hands of a newly-blind pianist, to touch the notes that would identify the tune. Slowly I began to map the territory of my hurts.

A door had been closed to me. I was still on the wrong side of this door, banging on it and screaming for someone to open it. On the other side of that door were people that had been in court. In my thoughts they held a picture of a murderer and papers upon which were written the story of the death of my son. These were the demons that sneaked about in my dreams, whispering things that I could never quite hear.

Before I could learn to live with my grief, I had to open that door. I had been dismissed from the process that dealt with the aftermath of the murder of my son. I had been hauled to his body to identify it, but prevented from ensuring that a kiss was placed upon it. I had been sent out from the mortuary, like a stray dog from a kitchen. I had been shamed by my poverty as he waited in his coffin. I had been banned from courtrooms so that the murderer did not have to show me his face. During the trial I had been excluded from the people involved in the trial as they grouped together under the banner of medical practitioners and their families. They had given information that misdirected and misinformed. I felt that there was something that they kept hidden, some secret they would not tell. They had power and they had exercised that power. I had none and they closed the door on me.

●   ●   ●

I understood that people may have concerns about talking openly in court. They were giving evidence and they would be careful about what they said. They would, I believed, be more forthcoming if the information were just being offered to help a grieving mother. I needed some answers. I would ask for them and put the demons to rest. I wrote to the Powys Health Trust and requested a meeting. I asked to have a meeting with all the staff involved with Andrew Cole and explained that I needed to make sense of this tragedy because the trial had left so many unanswered questions. The reply came. It told me that the complaint was duly noted, that they would try to facilitate this and that if I needed help, I could go to the Community Health Council.

I did need help. I recognised that I needed help. I made an appointment with the CHC in Newtown. On the day I walked in there I had nothing left. I had no self-respect, no dignity, and no strength. I walked into the building and made my way to the reception desk, expecting to be made to wait, to feel a nuisance and to be sent back out. I was met by Liz Lloyd. She smiled at me, a warm and honest smile. She guessed who I was and offered me tea or coffee. She introduced me to the chief officer, Jane Jeffs. She introduced me as though she were introducing someone who mattered, someone who was important to them. Jane was dressed in smart clothes that reflected her position, but the woman inside those clothes denied any superiority or intimidation. Her kind face, beneath the groomed fair hair, smiled a concerned smile. She was quiet but encouraging as I spoke. She wanted to hear what I had to say. She took notes as I spoke. She was not in a hurry. She did not look at the clock. She wanted to know what had happened. I poured my story out.

Jane said that she would write to the Powys Health Trust. She made sure that she had all the information she needed and a list of all the questions I wanted answers to. She said that she would write to Hereford, too. She asked me to confirm that she had all the necessary information. From that day, I had the help I needed. The respect they showed for me gave me back my self-respect. The strength they demonstrated as they fought for me gave me back my strength and the dignity with which they fought for me gave me back my dignity.

Our battle began. Jane Jeffs started writing. We fought with Hereford Hospital and Powys Health Trust. We challenged Victim Support, the Criminal Injuries Compensation Authority and the undertaker. We took on the Powys coroner, Dyfed Health Authority and the Welsh Office. Our fight has been going on for years. It involves the Home Office, the Lord Chancellor's Department (which has now changed its name to the Department of Constitutional Affairs) and the Prime Minister's Office. We've shared victories and defeats. Some issues have been resolved and some apologies have been accepted. Still, we fight on. If I was fighting alone or if I was doing this just for myself, I'd have given up a long time ago. I'm doing it to change the system. I'm fighting the system. I want to make things easier for other families of victims of murder and manslaughter. I want them to get better treatment. I can't change things for my family and I can't change things for William but I can do it for other people who are coming along behind. It will be William's legacy to them. It will be a kind of justice. That's what I'm fighting to achieve. Justice, I want justice for William.'

●　　●　　●

I took at a look at what had been Wendy's pristine front room. The day had taken its toll on it. It was strewn with papers. There were trial transcripts, letters, reports and the like. We had spent all day rummaging through two huge boxes of paperwork, alternating between shocked silences, vocal reactions and asking a host of questions. We'd smoked and snacked and made countless cups of tea. Jo and I were quite efficient in Wendy's kitchen by now and we just wandered to the kettle without asking. Dinner had been produced, admired and eaten several hours ago. Wendy-Lou wandered between her bedroom and the living room, sometimes joining in, sometimes getting things organized in the kitchen and sometimes laughing at the length of our intense gossip and the heap of cigarette ends sitting in the ash trays. I knew I still didn't have the whole story, but I had enough to be going on with. Jo knew much more than I did, but she hadn't heard it all at one telling before.

On the way home, the roads were as quiet as we were and I drove in a white knuckled silence, feeling drained by Wendy's tale. I had promised her, several times, that things would be different in Huddersfield.

I nursed a feeling of guilt and Jo was possibly feeling the same way. It was the way you feel when you go through passport control in some high security airport. You know you haven't got any intention of hi-jacking the 'plane but you worry that you are harbouring inappropriate thoughts and are about to be discovered by the staff. I wondered where my guilt was coming from now. It was definitely to do with thoughts that I might be harbouring. I had felt a twinge of anxiety that Wendy might be able to hear those thoughts. They had come in sneaky little whispers whilst I was at Wendy's house. I had drowned them out with empathy and support. They could whisper a little louder, now that I had managed to leave her house without being discovered. I could admit it to myself, now.

I was glad it wasn't me - glad it wasn't one of *my* children. I might be feeling hugely supportive of Wendy but I wouldn't have swapped places with her. Jo was deep in thought also. Jo has three sons. Finally, I broke the silence.

'I'm glad it wasn't one of my kids.'

'I know what you mean. I'm glad it wasn't one of mine, either,' Jo replied after one huge deep breath.

CHAPTER 12

A Goodbye Kiss

It was November and Wendy was having a busy month. The house was earmarked for demolition and, if she and Wendy-Lou could sit it out until then, they would be re-housed and have a relocation grant to help them with decorating the new house. It was becoming impossible for them to wait. There had been another attempt to break into the house, but this time it was unsuccessful. Three young men, who thought themselves gangsters, had taken to walking past the house at regular intervals and one of them carried a stick. The three of them stared at the window in a threatening manner. It seemed they were letting Wendy and Wendy-Lou know that they should not have called the police. As more and more people moved off the estate and more houses became boarded up, the area was becoming a playground for young thugs.

I think they sensed a power vacuum. I think they felt that the area was being abandoned, nobody cared about it and nobody was in control. Into this gap they strutted. They had power. Perhaps this would be the pinnacle of each of their careers. They had their day, for once in their lives they were kings of the world. I tried to imagine what it would be like to be them, but I could only see a dilapidated housing estate with boarded-up windows, overgrown gardens, broken fences and litter blowing in a weary breeze. If this was it, if this was as good as it got in their lives, they didn't have very much to look forward to.

Wendy and Wendy-Lou went to the Housing Department. They took with them a letter, supporting their application for a move, from Victim Support in Huddersfield. They waited in line and were then interviewed by a Housing Officer, Liam McParland. Wendy told him their story. She explained why they had moved up to Huddersfield. She told him about the burglary and the attempted burglary, she described the intimidating atmosphere that pervaded the street where she lived. She explained how stressful this situation was to them.

'When I am stressed, I put weight on. When she is stressed, she loses weight.' She pointed to Wendy-Lou, who was tinier than ever. 'Look at us. We look like Little and Large.' He looked at them. He listened to them. He accepted them as homeless and told them that he would work out how many points they had and send the information to them in writing. They both came out with smiles on their faces. They wouldn't be moving tomorrow or the next day. They would have to wait but they had been heard. Someone had listened to them and taken them seriously. Wendy was used to her words falling on deaf ears. She was used to being dismissed. Today she had told her story and it had been taken seriously. Their needs had been acknowledged.

'See, I told you things would be different now that you're in Huddersfield,' I said down the telephone, sounding smug, but secretly thinking, 'Thank you, Liam McParland, thank you for showing these women a bit of humanity.'

I next rang Wendy after the second funeral. I wanted to know how the day had gone. It's an awkward question to ask. How do you put it? 'Was the funeral good?' 'Did you enjoy the funeral?' I didn't want to sound as though I were asking about a holiday. I avoided all mention of the word 'funeral' and opted for 'How did it go then?' Wendy was happy to talk about it. She decided that the organ retention was a double edged sword. It had given them another chance to say goodbye to William.

She had let her instincts guide her, as she usually did, when choosing a funeral director. She had simply looked in Yellow Pages, let her eyes scroll down the list until they rested upon 'Taylor' and then she dialled the number. She started to explain, haltingly. The voice at the other end of the telephone asked her if she would like to talk on the telephone or if she would prefer someone to come to her house and talk to her. Wendy felt that she would find it easier to talk to someone, face-to-face and opted for the home visit.

A pleasant, handsome Yorkshireman called Tony kept the appointment. They drank tea together, while Wendy explained that her son's organs had been retained. She would be getting the organs back and wanted them, along with his ashes, to be buried in a proper grave in Warrington. She didn't have a date in mind for the funeral because she didn't know how long it would be before the organs were returned from Cardiff.

Tony was unhurried and a good listener. This must have been a most unusual set of circumstances for him to be presented with. The ashes were in Huddersfield, the organs in Cardiff and the burial was to be in Warrington. He let Wendy explain some more and interrupted only when Wendy referred to the battle that was the first funeral. He wanted to know what went wrong. Wendy felt so comfortable talking to him that she told him the whole story. He made no comment about the first funeral director but she could see by the expression on his face that he was unhappy with how they had been treated. He said that he would call again, with catalogues, so that they could choose the flowers.

So began a series of visits from the funeral director, who assured Wendy that all was under control. Wendy was determined that William's ashes and organs would be re-united in his coffin, making him whole again. She didn't want a tiny coffin, though. 'Don't put him in a baby's coffin. My boy was eighteen years old' she told him.

Once a release date for the organs was arranged, Tony called in to say that he was taking a funeral car down to Cardiff, in order to collect William and bring him to Huddersfield. He needed to make arrangements to take the ashes.

Wendy-Lou suddenly realised that she was to be parted from the precious casket and burst into tears. She didn't want William to go. Tony promised her that he would leave the ashes with them as long as he could. He would also return the casket to Wendy-Lou so that she could keep her memories of William in it. After collecting William's organs, which he only ever referred to as 'William', he arrived in a gleaming car to collect the casket. He carried it out to the car with great dignity and placed it on the passenger seat. He pulled the seat belt around and clasped it shut, as though his passenger were a living person.

Later that day he rang Wendy. He told her that he was having difficulty opening the casket. It had been sealed shut. 'I've never seen anything like it' he said. Wendy knew how upset Wendy-Lou would be if the casket were destroyed, but there was nothing else for it. She didn't want the ashes to be spilled. If the only way to get them out safely was by disregarding the condition of the casket, then so be it.

The following day Tony rang again. He told Wendy that his craftsman had stayed up most of the night in order to open the casket without damaging it. The ashes had been placed in the coffin along with the organs. The casket had been lined in white silk. He wanted to know if it was appropriate to return the casket when the coffin was brought to the house, later that day. He did not want Wendy-Lou to be upset more than she need be and was willing to return the casket another time, if that would be better. Wendy said that they would be delighted to receive the casket. She was overwhelmed to think of someone staying up, working hour after hour on the casket, just for them.

The evening before the funeral, William was brought home to his mum. He was carried into the front room in a five-foot coffin, one foot for each year that had passed since his death. Wendy and Wendy-Lou surrounded him with lighted candles and stayed up most of the night, playing his music and saying their goodbyes. Wendy-Lou placed letters and cards that had been sent to her from William inside the beautifully restored casket. It was to be her memory box.

The following morning the knock came upon the door. Wendy-Lou answered it and called to her mother, 'They're here, Mum.' 'Oh, I haven't finished listening to this song,' said Wendy, in reply, never meaning anyone else to hear her. Tony held up his hand. 'Stop,' he instructed his men. 'We'll wait here a moment or two until Wendy is ready to go.' Wendy was embarrassed, she hadn't intended to be heard but Tony insisted that they would wait until she was ready to leave.

An array of the most beautiful, creamy yellow roses was placed on the coffin lid and Tony gave Wendy a separate bunch of red roses to carry with her.

The coffin was carried out to the hearse and Tony showed Wendy that a pair of 'gates' had been made. They were designed to sit at the back of the hearse. They opened to allow the coffin to enter. The gates would be opened again to let William free. They were covered in primrose and blue flowers, the club colours of Warrington Rugby League, in memory of Bill, the hero of the hour at the first funeral. Wendy felt tears pricking at her eyes. Bill was also represented by means of a floral tribute to accompany his nephew's coffin.

Wendy and Wendy-Lou took their seats and the cars moved off. Wendy expected the car to pick up speed but it crawled away from the house. She wondered what was wrong and looked up. The cars were moving at walking pace behind Tony, who marched majestically before them, his head held high, proud to take William on his final journey.

The procession stopped before turning onto the main road to let Tony take his seat beside the driver of the hearse and they made their way to Warrington. Brian and Marc were waiting in Warrington. Christopher had been brought from prison, handcuffed and chained to a guard. The family were re-united for the day. Brian and Marc were coffin bearers, along with a close friend of Bill's, who was there to stand in for him and, with other family members, they lifted the coffin by the strong, weight-bearing handles and carried it inside.

The whole family and their friends were able to make the most of their second chance to say goodbye. It was five years since they had gathered together for the first funeral and on that occasion they had been in the early stages of shock. Today they were more composed. Wendy looked at her father, who had appeared at the first funeral, looking ashen and suddenly older than his years. Today his head was bowed in remembrance and his presence comforting.

The tears this day were warm and gentle, meeting hankies and quiet sniffs. The family were able to take comfort from each other and were united in a grief that had settled upon them like an old, familiar enemy. They were not rushed. At the graveside, Wendy, Brian, Marc, Christopher, Wendy-Lou and William's godmother, Kath each threw a red rose onto the coffin lid and said, 'Goodbye William, we love you.' From now on, they would always associate roses with this day. This beautiful image, that was to remain with them, was able to soothe some of the earlier hurts that had been imposed upon them.

The driver of the car that was to carry Wendy and Wendy-Lou back to Huddersfield was instructed to wait for them while the two women went to take refreshments that had been prepared by Wendy's mum. He sat outside to wait and refused the first invitation to come and take tea but was persuaded to join the family and friends. He never looked at the clock or tried to hurry them but joined them and listened to the family reflecting on how well the occasion had gone and how much better they all felt.

Eventually they returned to Huddersfield and were taken to their door. This had been the goodbye that had initially been denied to them. It had been a long wait but William had finally received his goodbye kiss.

CHAPTER 13

Making Amends

Several weeks later, Wendy called me to tell me that a meeting had been arranged in Huddersfield between Jane Jeffs, Dr Leadbeater and herself. She said that she would like me to accompany her. Dr Leadbeater, she explained, was the Home Office pathologist who had carried out the first post-mortem on William. I quickly agreed and went to Wendy's house earlier than need be, so that I could find out what the nature of the meeting was. This needed some explanation as communications between Wendy and Dr Leadbeater had been ongoing for quite some time.

●　　●　　●

Shortly after the first trial, Jane Jeffs had written to Hereford Hospital - as agreed with Wendy - and a meeting had been arranged. One of the issues that Wendy wished to explore was that of William being described as 'infected'. She wanted to know why Brian had not been allowed to kiss him and why they had been directed to have William cremated rather than interred. They were told to seek the answers from the Home Office pathologist, who was not under their authority. Jane Jeffs wrote to him and asked why William's body had been classed as a 'risk of infection' explaining that, as a result of this, Brian was pulled away from William's body when he bent over to kiss him and that the undertaker had told the family that William must be cremated, adding that this had caused lasting grief for the family.

Dr Leadbeater had replied, asking for clarification that Wendy was the next of kin. Once he was satisfied about this, he asked if she was the executor of the estate. Wendy went to Liverpool to be made the executor of estate, just so she could find answers to her questions. Dr. Leadbeater then wrote to say that he still could not give Wendy the information due to concerns about confidentiality, in that he had no way of knowing whether or not William would have wanted the information to be given out.

It was a brick wall. They could go no further and Wendy sensed that her anxieties were being dismissed. Her time and effort had been wasted, her trip to Liverpool futile. She seethed with frustration and anger. This man had information about her son. After his death, William had been treated like a leper. He mustn't be touched, mustn't be kissed, seal him up and burn him. She needed to know who had given these orders and why. Dr. Leadbeater would not tell her and she had to live with that frustration. Years passed before there was any more contact between them. Contact resumed after Sue telephoned Wendy to ask her if she had been watching the local news. It was at the time when the Alder Hey scandal broke concerning the misuse of body tissue. Sue had seen the television coverage and feared that Wendy may have been watching and worrying about William. Sue telephoned Hereford Hospital to ask if any organs belonging to William had been retained. They told her that this had not happened and Sue then rang Wendy to tell her everything she had heard.

Wendy was not convinced. She had sensed that something was wrong, right from the start. Faced with the thought that something of William's may have been retained, Wendy became convinced that they had kept his heart, so she rang Hereford Hospital herself. They told her that Dr Leadbeater worked at the University of Wales Hospital and had total responsibility for William while he was in Hereford. They did not believe that anything had been retained, however, and told her 'not to worry'. But Wendy was worried. She rang the Community Health Council. Jane Jeffs had recently moved on to another job, working on a review of Coroner Service, following various complaints about it. But they contacted Jane and Jane rang Wendy, promising 'to look into the matter and get back in touch'. As ever, Jane kept her promise and it wasn't long before she rang again to ask Wendy if she could attend a meeting with Dr Leadbeater and herself in Mold. It was to be held in the evening and overnight accommodation in a hotel for Wendy could be arranged. Of course, she agreed to go.

Wendy was not used to being booked into hotels for the night. She decided that this must be a sign that all was not well and she was to be given bad news. She decided that she would go to the meeting well-prepared and contacted the Organ Retention Group in Liverpool, who were dealing with the families of the Alder Hey victims. Wendy was advised to ask about 'blocks' and 'slides'. She was told that if organs had been retained she could expect the doctor to tell her that he had taken blocks and slides, but that these were only very thin slivers of tissue. What the doctor would not tell her, she was told, was that he probably took one hundred and fifty or so of them, a whole organ.

Armed with this knowledge, Wendy travelled to Mold and found her hotel. She went up to her room to unpack her overnight things and was sorting herself out when the telephone in her room rang. It was Jane, announcing her arrival. Wendy went downstairs to meet her and the two women hugged. They went off for a coffee so that they could catch up with each other's news. Jane was delighted to discover that Wendy was no longer looking for a table with an ash tray. She had given up smoking six months before.

● ● ●

That evening, at the appointed time, they went to the meeting room and Wendy finally came face to face with Dr Leadbeater. She explained, as clearly as she could, how it had felt to be told that they were not allowed to kiss William. He listened to her and apologised for the dismissive letters that she had received from him. Wendy could tell that his apology was genuine. She could tell by the tone of his voice, the look in his eyes and his body language that this man was taking her seriously, treating her with respect. He was a decent man, a man of honesty and integrity. She accepted his apology, understanding that bureaucracy often ties people into a system that takes no account of individual circumstances and prevents them from engaging with members of the public in a compassionate manner. Dr Leadbeater then told Wendy that some organs *had* been retained. At that point Wendy declared that she needed to go outside for a cigarette. She left the room and Jane followed.

Outside, she closed her eyes and saw an image of a hand reaching into William's body and plucking out his heart. She asked a passer-by for a cigarette, explaining that she had given up smoking but she had just received some bad news. Gratefully, she took the cigarette and the light, sucked in a great lung full of smoke and swallowed on her tears. Jane stayed by her, a comforting and reassuring presence while she smoked.

Wendy returned to the meeting room and told Dr Leadbeater that she did not want any more information at that point because she was unable to deal with it. She told him that, if he wished to make amends for his small part in the tragedy, he should make sure that what they had of William was returned to her as quickly as possible. He said that he would have to get permission but that he did not envisage there would be any problem with that. He would sort it out. Wendy told him that she didn't blame him, he was just doing his job but she blamed the system that allowed it to happen.

Jane took Wendy out for a meal and debriefing session. She never allowed Wendy to leave any meeting without going for a coffee and talking over what had been said, how Wendy felt and what their next move ought to be. During the meal, Jane told Wendy that Dr Leadbeater had asked her to inform Wendy that he would be available in the morning if there was anything else that she would like to ask. It was a kind gesture, but Wendy just wanted to get home.

A further meeting was arranged not long afterwards in Cardiff. Wendy's experience, feelings and opinions were to be included in an Organ Advisory Document, along with those of other families. Wendy, Jane and Dr Leadbeater gathered in a meeting room. Wendy told him that she was ready to be told what organs had been retained. Dr. Leadbeater carefully placed a case on the table, flipped open the catches and said, 'I can do better than that, I can show you.'

'NO!' screamed Wendy and Jane, clinging on to each other in horror. Dr. Leadbeater looked at them from over the top of the case, 'Oh no, nothing like that,' he said, taken aback, 'what I have here is the paperwork.'

With a good deal of sensitivity, he talked about blocks and slides. He explained that he had retained nothing of William's heart or brain. He also showed them the toxicology reports. He had taken samples of William's blood and hair. William had no trace of alcohol or drugs in his body. Jane looked at Wendy with a huge smile on her face. It was what Wendy had been waiting to hear. If William had even smoked cannabis at any time in the last six months before his death, traces of it would have been identified in the sample of his hair. William had, as he had assured his mum, been successful at the Detox Unit , where he was undergoing rehabilitation, in Cardiff. He was clean as a whistle.

A police officer had told Dr. Leadbeater that William was a drug addict. There were concerns about hepatitis and other blood infections. Because of this, Dr Leadbeater had warned the mortuary assistant that the body was infected. Nobody had bothered to check if the police officer knew what he was talking about. He didn't. It was an ill-informed, judgemental remark. But because of it William had become untouchable. His family had been deprived of physical contact. William had been sealed within a coffin and cremated. His family would carry those scars for the rest of their lives.

Dr Leadbeater told Wendy that he had arranged for the University of Wales Hospital to pay for a modest funeral. If there were any problems encountered with that, he would sort it out himself. This was a man who knew how to make amends and I looked forward to meeting him.

● ● ●

Jane arrived at the house to pick us up. She was just as Wendy had described, smart without being intimidating and with a kindness of heart that shone out of her. We arrived at the meeting room. Wendy shook Dr Leadbeater's hand and I heard her thank him for giving her family a chance to say goodbye to William in a way that had made them all feel so much better.

Dr. Leadbeater explained that he had not been called to give evidence in either the first or the second trial. He had been surprised about this but the Home Office employed very few pathologists, they were busy and if he was not called to give evidence he did not attend trials. Had he been called to the witness box he would have told the court that William had no trace of drugs or alcohol in his body. He would also have explained the nature of his injuries. There were stab wounds around William's genitalia, but the murderer had not cut off his penis. He also talked about the jewellery. William had a ring in his navel but he did not remember any other jewellery and he always made notes about any jewellery on bodies when writing the post mortem report. He had noted the ring in William's navel in his report.

There were twelve stab wounds to William's back, ranging in size from ten centimetres to two centimetres. There were two stab wounds to his left buttock and another two on the junction between his neck and back. Of the forty stab wounds that had been inflicted on William, sixteen would be visible while he was lying on his front.

Warm farewells were said. There was no need for Jane to take Wendy for a coffee this time, Wendy was happy with what she had heard and I was there to listen. We walked away and I noticed that Wendy still had a smile on her face. I looked at her quizzically and she told me that, for the last five years, she had believed her son had been sexually mutilated. The news that this was untrue had given her a good feeling. Dr Leadbeater, I thought, was very, very good at making amends.

●　　●　　●

I read a copy of the report when it came out. It had a frightening title: 'Post Mortem Examination and the Removal and Retention of Organs and Tissue: A Public Consultation Exercise'. Within its daunting cover it was surprisingly readable and I could see Wendy's comments all over it, although it mentioned no names. There was advice on breaking the news of a death by murder or manslaughter to the relatives. It was essential to use the word 'dead' rather than platitudes such as 'nothing could be done for...' When relatives are in shock, communication must leave no room for misinterpretation. Relatives should be provided with every scrap of information possible, but it must be provided to them sensitively and certainly before it is provided to the media. When relatives are transported to hospitals, they must not be required to wait in public waiting rooms - every effort should be made to find them a private room. Once all trace evidence has been removed from a body, there should be no barrier to touching or holding the body. A coroner does not need the relative's permission to retain material that bears upon the cause of death but, in future, relatives must at least be informed of what is to be retained and formal audited systems must be put in place to record and monitor retained material.

One part of the report described what I had discovered in my conversations with Wendy. 'The police officers involved need to maintain awareness of the fragility of the bereaved relatives' feelings and the fact that relatives will always be able to recall with alarming clarity every second of that meeting. Those memories include the recollection of every casual remark that was made, certainly long after the police officers have forgotten about them.' This was something that I had found quite disconcerting. Wendy remembered events and conversations surrounding the murder and its aftermath with total recall. She explained to me that these things are 'burned upon your brain so that you can never forget them'. I think that is an important lesson for all professionals to learn in their dealings with the relatives of murder and manslaughter. Whatever they do or say will be remembered by the people they are dealing with for the rest of their lives, who will replay it over and over again. They will repeat it, precisely and accurately, many times. One day it might end up in a book.

Wendy never wanted to sue anybody. She never sought financial reward from any agency. The fear that has been created by our litigious society has caused professionals to build barriers. When Wendy was able to breach those barriers, she had as much to offer as she had to gain. If someone had made a mistake, she wanted them to apologise, make amends and learn from the experience. In turn, Dr Leadbeater gained as much from Wendy as she gained from him. He developed an awareness of how his work impacted upon the relatives that he had never before come into contact with. He is now able to pass this information on to others within the system and improve that system for those families who have yet to come into contact with it. That is why Wendy won't shut up, why she won't give in. She has said many times that she is 'fighting the system' and I used to think that she meant she was some sort of anarchist. That isn't what she means, though. She means that she is breaking down barriers and persuading people to listen. They will learn from what she has to say and the system will change.

The system is people. It is us. Wendy is fighting for 'all those families who are coming on behind'. They are people, they are us. We don't know who they are yet. They could be anybody. Murder is indiscriminate. Every year, approximately eight hundred families will become the relatives of a victim of murder or manslaughter. They may never know that someone has been fighting for them. She's often faced criticism from people, both personally and professionally.

Some people think Wendy should get over it and put it behind her. Some people think she should shut up and get on with her life. I don't.

CHAPTER 14

Sharing Success

One or two changes were happening in my life as that winter was being elbowed out of the way by the spring of 2002. I was aware that my contract would soon be at an end and I needed to think about the next job. I spotted an advertisement for Witness Service Manager (part of Victim Support) at Huddersfield Magistrates' Court. It really appealed to me. The Court Witness Service had been running at all Crown Court centres for some years. It had proved successful and the Government had therefore decided that it should now be made available in all magistrates' courts across England and Wales by the end of March.

The application pack thudded onto the floor as it dropped through the letterbox. This had been the biggest shock to me when I re-entered the job market. Application forms were much shorter when I left school. Employers wanted to know your name and address, qualifications, work experience and hobbies. They explained what the job was all about when you went to the interview and decided whether they liked you or not on the spot. Things were different in the office environment then also. Most employees had ashtrays on their desks and as a junior I was often sent out to buy cigarettes and sandwiches. If you got things wrong, someone would shout at you. I remember it as being so much simpler.

●　　　●　　　●

In today's job market, application packs come in enormous envelopes stuffed full of leaflets that take hours to read. Application forms ask for page after page of information and interviews would be better described as auditions. I work on the basis that the idea is to try and work out what they are looking for and then tell them what they want to hear. The first part of the process is a conundrum. You need to wade through all the bumf and work out 'who you need to be'. Then you can pick out all the relevant bits of experience from your previous jobs and personal life in order to create that person and present the information on the application form. If an interview is offered, I go along and perform in the persona I have. It's method acting - and I always get terrible stage fright before an interview.

Employers often end up with closet Thespians, liars and cheats in their employ, because these are the applicants who often have the best chance of getting though the process. I'm a bit of all three. I've been prepared to be less than honest in order to get the jobs that I have really wanted. The Court Witness Service wanted to know my complete employment history, every job that I ever had in my life. The truth is that I can't remember them all. I left school at sixteen. It was 1969. I have no idea why it is important to an employer to know what a middle-aged woman was doing back then and I didn't think it would do my chances of employment any good to explain it!

I would have had to put my teenage years into context. I was born into a world that had been ravaged by the Second World War. When I arrived, in 1953, my mum was issued with my ration book and actually used some of the coupons before rationing finally ended. We lived in the beautiful countryside of West Yorkshire, next door to my maternal grandparents. I tottered around after my grandad and watched him carry his three-legged milking stool out to the cows and squirt the milk into a bucket. We had hens in the yard, a beautiful cart horse called Bonny and my brother and I made pets of the farm animals. I watched the fields in front of our house change from brown to green to gold as the seasons changed. I lay on my back in the moorland grass behind our house and listened to skylarks soaring across a blue sky.

It was a sparsely populated area, so it was most convenient for me that our neighbour, Mrs. Haigh, gave birth to a baby girl, Mary, six months after I was born. Mary and I wandered about in woods and fields with a freedom that is rare today. I found the world a pretty place, full of trees, flowers and animals. My mum grew Red Hot Pokers and lupins in the garden. I remember that they were beautiful, towering things surrounded by greedy insects. I have always been disappointed with the specimens I have grown, but I must accept that they are never going to look as magnificent again as they did when I was two and half feet tall. The world I was growing up in was peaceful, pretty and safe.

My paternal grandad was a great story teller. I loved listening to him. As I grew older, I became curious about photographs and demanded information about the wars that had put my grandfathers and father into military uniforms. I listened to my grandad's stories about the trenches, how rats would run ahead of the thick rolling clouds of mustard gas and he had to get himself covered-up before the gas reached him because it burned any flesh it came into contact with. My dad gave me and my brother his medals to play with because he didn't want them. They weren't much fun so we buried them. We decided that someone, some day would dig them up and think they had found buried treasure but they would be hugely disappointed when they found out that they had only uncovered our dad's medals. I don't know why he held on to the Burma Star but I have it now and still haven't buried it.

I was just nine years old when President John Kennedy decided it would be okay to risk starting World War Three. I don't really remember the Cuban Missile Crisis but some of the fear that it generated must have entered my thinking. By the time I was twelve years old, the American troops were gathering in Vietnam and it wasn't long before we saw pictures of the emerging horror on television screens in our own front rooms. At school we were taken into a classroom and shown a film about nuclear war. It was called 'The War Game' and was banned from television screens. It explained in graphic detail what would happen when the next war started.

The result of all this was that I never expected to grow old. From my point of view, it came as a bit of a shock to discover that my lovely world of changing seasons and blue skies was run by crackpots who kept declaring war.

It was the late 'sixties. I was in my teens. I didn't like how the planet was run and the fact that I was going to die in a nuclear war before I got much older. There didn't seem much point in planning an interesting career path and engaging with healthy living. It made a lot more sense to wear purple loon pants, read Ken Kesey, listen to Roy Harper and stay up all night with like-minded young people, getting stoned.

So it was that my early years were not clearly directed on a suitable career path and that my memory of them is sometimes hazy. It was a lot of fun, though. The legacy of these early years is not too difficult to spot. I can (and do) still sing along to all the songs on 'Flat Baroque and Berserk'. I read the legend 'Smoking Kills' on cigarette packs and feel an urge to add underneath in a scrawl, 'So do wars. Sort yourselves out and then you can start lecturing me!' and post it off to the House of Commons.

So how is all this going to look on an application form for a job in a magistrates' court? How should I summarise it?: 'I can't really recall all my movements during my late-teens and early-twenties because it was all a bit chaotic and not easy to explain to people who don't know where the inspiration for all those psychedelic posters came from. I thought my charred remains were going to be covered with about three feet of radio-active dust by now but seeing as we're all still here, I decided that I'd like to do something interesting in order to earn my living'.

I find it a lot easier to say I spent those years working in a nice little book shop in Clifton that closed down in 1982. The owner was a lovely old man. I probably kept in touch with him, just Christmas cards and the annual letter, until his death in 1993. This is the persona that attends interviews for me. Someone nice, someone quiet, someone who doesn't ask awkward questions and who makes a good impression on any potential employer. Then, when the interview is over, I can step outside, roll a fag and walk off singing, 'I've got a brother and he's one year old, he wears a zappy little nappy...'

I got the job and the three day training programme started in early March. It was a permanent contract. I finally had a job without an end date! I bought my council house. I'd lived in it for seven years when I took possession of the property, along with a mortgage that was reasonable enough not to keep me awake at night.

There had never been a Court Witness Service at Huddersfield Magistrates' Court. I was a pioneer, establishing the service right from the start. It was my baby. I loved it and I learned a lot about court processes. I was required to recruit, train and manage a team of volunteers who would support and prepare witnesses to give evidence. It was one of those rare jobs which offer a huge amount of job satisfaction. Sometimes witnesses would give me a big hug and thank me before they left the court. In the years that I worked there, I never took a day off sick and I always gave my best efforts. I hope I have exonerated myself for the 'little fictions' that appeared on my application form. If any future potential employer demands complete honesty, I shall have to create an application pack to rival the one they send me. I could make leaflets to be read in conjunction with the completed application form. In the space to be used for employment history I could give a cross reference: 'For employment history during my early years, read leaflet 1969A – Hitler, JFK and the Apparent Futility of a Superannuated Pension Scheme.'

●   ●   ●

Meanwhile, Wendy was still waiting to move. She and Wendy-Lou had worked out a way of avoiding leaving the house unoccupied. When Wendy wanted to go out, Wendy-Lou would stay in with one of her friends and the dog. Wendy would be in when Wendy-Lou was out. They occasionally went to the supermarket together. It wasn't very far and they would make their purchases and then rush back home, hoping that the house was in the same state they left it. It was a state of siege.

In April, Wendy-Lou had to stay on guard while Wendy went to visit Hereford Hospital. I went to visit her, shortly after her return and we caught up with each other's news. She was pleased with her visit to Hereford and had to give me the background information so that I could understand why she was still smiling about it.

It hadn't been so much a battle with Hereford Hospital, more a skirmish, a little fracas to get her and Jane Jeffs fully match fit. Jane Jeffs had written to Hereford Hospital soon after meeting Wendy. She had a list of complaints to put to them. She wanted them to explain why Brian had not been able to kiss William goodbye, why they had been hurried out of the mortuary after the identification and why they weren't given another chance to say goodbye before William was sealed in his coffin. She wanted to know why Wendy and Brian had been taken to sit in a supermarket cafe while they waited to identify William. She wanted an explanation for the instruction given to the undertaker that William must be cremated rather than interred.

A meeting was arranged so that Wendy could meet the doctor who was in charge of the mortuary. John Hedges agreed to attend the meeting because he had witnessed the events and subsequent funeral arrangements. The meeting began without John Hedges, who had not shown up. Wendy and Jane were faced with a doctor who appeared to dismiss everything Wendy had to say. He denied that these things could have happened and explained to Wendy that she was in shock at the time and had no clear idea what was going on. Wendy was furious and told him that there was an independent witness. The doctor smirked at her, in what she thought was a contemptuous manner and pointed out that the independent witness had not attended. Before the sentence was completely out of his mouth, there was a knock on the door and John Hedges entered, apologising for being late. Wendy asked him to tell the doctor what he remembered and he confirmed everything that she had said without the benefit of having heard the early discussion in the meeting room.

The doctor's attitude changed when faced with this corroboration. He asked Wendy what was needed and they entered into a useful discussion. Afterwards, Jane took Wendy for a coffee in the hospital restaurant and asked what time it shut. She was told that it closed at five but the staff canteen was open all night, until the restaurant opened again at seven in the morning. She fired another letter off to point out that Wendy and Brian should have been directed to the canteen to wait, not taken to a supermarket.

Further letters were exchanged between Jane and staff at the hospital and another meeting held. Some matters were referred to the Home Office pathologist but what Wendy had to say about the services offered by the hospital mortuary were being accepted and there were promises that they would act upon the information. Wendy told them that visitors should have well-presented, private rooms, painted in calming colours, to wait in. They should be prepared for the experience of the identification of a loved one. They needed to be given all the necessary information to take away with them so that they could think about it again when they arrived home and plan a further visit if they so wished. They should be treated with the sensitivity they needed at such a time and never rushed. Wendy explained how all this could avoid adding to the trauma that people were suffering when they received the information that a loved one had become the victim of a sudden death, either in a road traffic accident or as a result of murder or manslaughter.

The Patient Affairs Officer expressed her gratitude to her for bringing the matters to attention, saying that, until Wendy spoke up, staff were unaware of the problems that mortuary arrangements were presenting for visitors.

Wendy told Jane that she would like to attend again in twelve months time, to see if they had fulfilled their promises. This was agreed, but events in Wendy's life overtook the visit. An appeal came along and then a second trial. Wendy forgot about the return visit to Hereford until the organ retention issue brought it back into her mind.

When Wendy's request to visit the hospital arrived, it was met with a welcoming response. The Patient Affairs Officer was delighted to receive the visit and proudly showed Wendy around. They had taken on board everything that Wendy had said. There were several waiting rooms available for families. The rooms had been painted in calming colours and fresh flowers were on display. Information leaflets were available for families to take away so that they could read them at home and be informed of their rights to come back to the mortuary and say goodbye to their loved one. Nobody was rushed and people were treated with respect and sensitivity.

We were pleased with ourselves that day. We had news of achievements to share. 'Have another biscuit,' said Wendy, offering me something with half a million calories in it. 'Mmmm, lovely,' I said, tucking in.

CHAPTER 15

Green of Grass and Blue of Sky

As warmer weather and sunshine arrived, I wanted to introduce Wendy to Castle Hill. I live within walking distance of it. The only bit of information I remember from my school geography lessons involves Castle Hill. Apparently, if you place a ruler on the map at right angles to the edge of the page (as though you are about to underline something) and draw a straight line across the flat landscape of East Yorkshire, the North Sea and The Netherlands, you won't meet a higher point until you hit the Ural Mountains in Russia. I've never done it and can't remember paying attention to the map when the teacher told us, but I'm sure it's true.

I could remember this because I was able to make the journey from Castle Hill to The Urals, inside my head, as the teacher described it. There are many things that you learn about yourself as you get older. I now know that my mind requires words and pictures before it can take information in. If I am listening to someone, I run the words in my head, with a cinematic sequence running in synchrony. If I can't run the film, I can't understand what is being said. I find directions very difficult, whether they concern routes or instructions on how to assemble flat-pack furniture. On the other hand, I once listened to one schizophrenic advise another how to get his voices under control and it made perfect sense. It involved the voices being locked inside a head, with no real experience of the outside world. The guy giving advice explained that you read a good science fiction book, becoming totally engrossed in the story. The voices have no way of knowing whether this journey into space is a fiction or a fact because they are locked in your head and can only see what you can see. You have to get so involved in the story that you can see the stars whizzing past, through the windows. You can see the crew members and the controls on the ship. At this point, you tell the voices in your head that you are the captain of this ship and if they start messing you about, the ship will soon be completely out of control and on course for a head-on collision with the next meteorite. They are immediately terrified and start behaving themselves. 'Yeah, works for me' I said, impressed, forgetting for a moment that I don't hear voices and was on a shift as relief manager in a probation and bail hostel, to supplement my student loan.

The down-side of this type of understanding was, for me, that I was completely out of my depth in maths and all the sciences. The numbers and letters just sat on the blackboard and I could find no way of engaging with them. The significance, regarding my friendship with Wendy, is that she has always been delighted that I listen to her, understand what she says and remember it. I do this because she communicates in a way that I can visualise. She paints pictures with her words and I can run my film as she speaks. Our communications are the foundation of our trust in each other. We have got to know each other through our anecdotal life histories. Through them, we reveal our experiences and our responses and reactions to them. This has shown us how much we share by way of our beliefs, values and judgement systems. We have a lot in common and generally crack up laughing at the same points of a story.

●　　●　　●

Castle Hill is a special place to me. I wanted to share it with Wendy. Looking back, I was putting her through an initiation. I wanted her to see Castle Hill through the eyes of a local. I wanted her to feel that it belonged to her in the way I feel that it belongs to me. It was a gift from me to her. I gave her chapter and verse on the subject as we made our way towards it. I explained that it was the site of an Iron Age hill fort and about how difficult it would be to sneak up on it. Local legend has it that it was the 'lair of a wyrm'. I suggested what the hill might look like with a great dragon rising from it. After the Norman Invasion, the De Lacy family built a castle on the top, giving the hill its name. When the castle eventually lay abandoned, the stone was removed and recycled, until by about the seventeenth century, nothing was left above ground level. 'You can't go leaving a castle lying about round here,' I told Wendy, 'somebody will soon shift it and make a bob or two.'

There are stories about secret tunnels running from under the hill and coming out miles away. The hill itself is 894 feet above sea level. To commemorate the jubilee of Queen Victoria, a 106 foot tall tower was built, bringing it up to a nice round 1,000 feet above sea level at its top. It is called Jubilee Tower but I have heard that Victoria Tower is the official name. During the Second World War, some fool suggested that the tower should be demolished because it was handy for German bombers to navigate by. Either everybody had grown too fond of the tower or nobody could be bothered to pull it down, or perhaps somebody reminded them that it cost over £3,000 to build, because it is still there today.

'I know I am home when I see Castle Hill in the distance,' I told Wendy, as I dragged her mercilessly up the hill. 'But the best thing is the view. From one side you see the town, from another, only countryside. You can see Holme Moss, Pole Moor and Emley Moor television mast,' I babbled on enthusiastically while she cursed her asthma and begged for a few moments to get her breath back.

I was still pointing at things and naming names when we reached the summit. 'Look, look over there, "Tensing". See! You can just see a bit of the stadium over there.' I pointed and directed her gaze at the slither of blue and white in the distance as though I were seeing the face of God. The problem with season ticket holders is that we think our stadium is Mecca and we expect everyone else to feel the same. It is not an unfamiliar sight to either of us, I both live and work within easy walking distance of Huddersfield Town's McAlpine Stadium but you'd think it was a glimpse of Camelot that I was offering her. For me, this was the home of Huddersfield Town AFC. For Wendy, it was where she went to watch men running around after an oval-shaped object. We may go there on seperate days but it was our stadium.

Wendy dare not be anything but impressed. She was quiet, but that might have been because she was having a bit of trouble getting her breath. She had the right sort of smile on her face, though. It was the sort of smile I imagine Siddhartha wore when he worked out that, for him, enlightenment came from within and he settled down to a fulfilled life as the ferryman, listening to the river. Castle Hill was the closest thing I could find to Siddhartha's river.

'There are usually people up here, flying kites or chucking Frisbees for dogs and kids on nice days,' I told her 'and they smile a lot. This is a happy place.'

We sat for a while on the way back down. Wendy gazed into the distance and then said, 'Look at that.'

'What?' I looked around.

'That grass over there,' she said, nodding her head in the direction that she was looking.

'What about it?' I asked.

'It's green,' she said.

'You're not kidding!' I replied with a voice that dripped sarcasm.

'Oh, no,' she said seriously. 'You don't understand. I haven't seen colour for years. Since the day William was murdered, the world has been black and white to me - monochrome, like an old film. Today I can see that the grass is green. You're right. Castle Hill is a special place.'

I was humbled by her words. I had bounced around all day like a mad salesman, pointing out all the landmarks, telling her all the stories about dragons and secret tunnels and getting her to suck the air into her lungs and feel how fresh it was. So busy was I with my enthusiasm that I had forgotten she needed none of it. We are surrounded by hills. There are loads of places to fly kites. People like going to Castle Hill, not because it is an available hill but because it is a good place to be. Wendy could feel it. She had just let herself bathe in the atmosphere and a chink of sunlight had broken through the cloud that cast her world into a land of shadow.

We sat for some time, while Wendy enjoyed the green of grass and I gazed possessively at the sky, secretly pledging that I would always know how it felt to have endless blue above my head.

CHAPTER 16

Taking the Stage

I was just about coming round from a long sulk in the summer of 2002, because Brentford had knocked Huddersfield Town out of the semi-finals of the play-offs in May. When the new fixture list came out, I was delighted to see that our first game of the season was at home to Brentford, who had gone on to lose in the play-off final. I may have said the words 'grudge' and 'match' in the same sentence. If I had known what was to come that season, I would have just gone to bed and had a little weep. Sometimes I think it is just as well that we don't know what's around the corner. I was in the process of cutting the fixture list out of the newspaper when the 'phone rang. It was Wendy.

'Hiya, Helen. What's Brockholes like?' she asked.

There was a twenty second silence while I contemplated what she said.

'Wendy, have you been offered a house in Brockholes?' I asked, hopefully. She had. I was delighted. I had lived in Brockholes many years ago. It was a rural village, near Holmfirth. It was an extremely fortunate opportunity to be allocated a local authority property in Brockholes. Tenants often bought their homes on the small estate, diminishing the stock of houses for let. It was quiet, peaceful. It would be just right.

Wendy and Wendy-Lou moved into the small, two bedroom house within the week. Wendy wandered around it and knew that she was home at last. By the time I went round to see the place she had scrubbed it, decorated it, had the carpets laid, a new sofa and chair delivered and made the place her own. I was almost suffocated in the tiny front room. She had chosen three different, and competing, reds with which to decorate. There was red paper on the walls, a red carpet on the floor and a beautiful sofa and chair in a third shade. Orangey-red, purple-red and rose-red gathered together and fought bitterly. Each would have looked fine without the other two. To brighten things up a bit, Wendy had papered one wall in bright, citrus-yellow. Wendy and I had a lot in common but we didn't share the same taste in household decor. I looked at her face. She had a smile like the Cheshire cat and a gentle glow in her usually-dull eyes. I felt my own smile widen to match hers and it didn't matter a damn what colours she had chosen, I just loved it.

She let me explore the house thoroughly before she told me that she had agreed to speak at a conference of professionals. I asked her if she was nervous and she admitted that she had a serious case of the jitters. She already had experience of public speaking. In the September of 1999 she had spoken at the All Wales Victim Support Conference at the University of Aberystwyth. She had been invited to give a short presentation on the support that she had received from Victim Support. Jane Jeffs had moved on to her new post and John Howard had taken over her role at the Community Health Council. John had given Wendy tremendous support and spent many hours of his own time helping her to practice the speech.

Tricia had supported her through the conference. Tricia was the Victim Support volunteer who had attended at Wendy's house on the day of the murder. Together they listened to speeches, attended workshops and enjoyed relaxation in the evenings. She ensured that Wendy enjoyed her time there, offering her genuine support and comfortable companionship. It was the first time that victims had been included in the conference and three of them were due to speak on the final morning, before the closing speeches. A victim of rape spoke about the support she had received, followed by a victim of mugging. Both were genuinely grateful.

Wendy took to the stage and looked into the audience, where Marc, Wendy-Lou and her sister, Sue, were sitting with Jane Jeffs. They had travelled to the conference for just that one morning, in order to support and listen to Wendy. 'Good morning, my name is Wendy. Are victims victimised?' she asked and looked down into the audience, at the faces of the many professionals who were seated comfortably, waiting for another plaudit from another grateful service user.

Wendy continued with her presentation and described the events that had followed the murder of her son. She watched the expressions on their faces change as the wait to identify William, in Safeway's cafe, was presented to them. By the time Wendy was telling them that, as the mother of a murdered son, she felt that she needed to ask if she had any rights at all, some members of the audience were shuffling uncomfortably in their seats. Wendy could not feel apologetic about offering them a challenging presentation. She felt it was vital that she highlight the insensitivities that she had suffered at the hands of some of the professionals with whom she had come into contact, in the aftermath of the murder. It would never be possible to achieve improvements in the system if nobody voiced concerns. It may have felt uncomfortable for them to hear these criticisms when they were expecting praise and gratitude but they needed to know that careless treatment of secondary victims left an indelible stain upon their souls. Although her complaint had been treated with all due respect and seriousness, it was not enough to offer closer supervision to one member of staff. She wanted them to make sure that this was never allowed to happen again. It was vital to Wendy that they understood she was fighting for better treatment of such victims, that the trauma of the loss of a loved one to murder could devastate families. She was fighting the cause and had even been obliged to extend that fight to the organization whose job it was to support those families. She offered her criticisms on behalf of all those families coming along behind. She hoped that they would benefit from what she had to say.

Jane Jeffs was terribly proud of Wendy and made herself equally 'popular' by writing to Victim Support and telling them that she was disappointed to note they had left the presentations of the victims until last, when a large proportion of the potential audience had already gone home.

• • •

'The Aberystwyth presentation is out of date now,' Wendy told me. 'Would you help me to update it?' I read the worn copy that she handed to me and longed to do something radical with it. I sometimes imagined that I had forgotten everything I had been taught at university but years of engaging with a close, textual analysis of the written word had left its mark. There is a time and a place for literary criticism. This wasn't it.

'Okay. Can you give me a bit more information about your audience? What do you want to say and why?'

Wendy explained that the conference had been arranged in order to gather information designed to impact upon *Victim's Charter* work that the Government were engaged in. It had been organized by the Home Office and the audience would include representatives of several agencies. There would be professionals there from the National Probation Service, Victim Support, Crown Prosecution Service, the police and doctors.

'Doctors,' repeated Wendy, 'I've got things that I want to say to doctors who work in the Criminal Justice System.' The look on her face always suggested that she would like to round them up and incarcerate them somewhere very uncomfortable for a few years when she mentioned doctors. I was glad I had never been tempted to study medicine. We needed to empty the box of papers all over the new carpet and isolate some of the documentation.

'The appeal,' said Wendy as she pulled out a modest-sized document. 'The second trial,' she announced pointing to a much thicker bundle of paperwork. 'Letters, letters, no. No. No. Oh, yes letter ... letter, yes and the Independent Review.' Wendy continued with her sorting out as I watched documents be spoken to in either dismissive or triumphant terms. 'The Ombudsman's Report,' she finally announced to the obese document that had arrived the week before and had been read several times already. 'Letters, No' were put back into the storage box and 'Letters, Yes' were incorporated into an impressive stack, along with the transcripts and reports. I use the same filing system myself, officially known as the 'collect it all together in one place and then spend hours rummaging through it until you either find the document you want or stop caring about where it is' system as used in many homes and workplaces around the country.

I didn't have time to stay and listen to the whole story from Wendy so she gave me a quick guided tour of the paperwork, transferred them to a plastic carrier bag and let me take them home to read the story for myself. Wendy had told me bits here and there. She had often complained about the behaviour of the doctors in the case of *Regina v. Andrew Douglas Cole*, but, if I was going to write a presentation for her, I needed every detail to hand.

I started with the appeal, as per instructions and made cross-references to the Ombudsman's Report and a letter from the Chief Executive of Powys Health Care NHS Trust, so that I had the complete picture. Between them, the papers told an appalling story.

During the trial, Andrew Cole had become upset when the photographs of William and Fiona were being shown to the court. He had been taken to the cells 'howling' as it was worded in the transcript. I remembered Wendy telling me about that. I remembered also, that Dr Foy had gone down to the cells to ascertain if Cole was fit to continue giving evidence. She had assured the court that he was and the trial had continued. When the trial was over and Cole was found guilty of murder, Dr Foy was shocked. She expected him to be found guilty of manslaughter. Off she went, to the defence solicitor and prepared an affidavit, explaining that she had given evidence suggesting that there was no sign of violence in Cole's history before he stabbed two people to death. However, when she went down to the cells to see him, she felt for the first time that he was dangerous and she was frightened of him.

Christopher Pitchford QC submitted in evidence that the material in Dr Foy's affidavit was such as to render the jury's verdict unsafe. He invited the Court, if it accepted the submission, to either substitute a verdict of manslaughter or submit the case for retrial.

Lord Thomas argued that the information detailed in the affidavit should not affect the safety of the conviction. Dr Foy's opinion had not been, to any significant extent, canvassed before the jury and her evidence as to the history of Cole's treatment at Talgarth could not now be different from that which it was during the trial.

The appeal was allowed. The conviction for murder was quashed. Cole was an innocent man and transferred to the remand wing at his prison to await a fresh trial.

•   •   •

As per Wendy's instructions, I also took a close look at a letter from Powys Health Care NHS Trust. It was dated 21 May 1999 and was a final report on the action taken by the Trust, following the complaint that Wendy had made. Number 5 on their list read 'As stated before, the records in this case were removed illegally without the permission of the Trust. They were eventually located and returned to the safe keeping of the Trust.'

The Ombudsman's report described how the medical records were retained by the Associate Specialist and the Consultant. I knew from the trial transcript that Dr Foy was the Associate Specialist and Dr Hessian was the Consultant.

I went to bed and wished I had not started reading Wendy's papers that night. Now I couldn't get to sleep. I kept thinking about Dr Foy. She didn't like the verdict so it seems that she took steps that resulted in them having to start all over again. She was asked about the welfare of Cole during the trial. She informed the court that he was fit to continue giving evidence. She did not express any concerns at that time. She therefore allowed her patient (she was the doctor responsible for Andrew Cole's treatment while he was in Talgarth Hospital) to give evidence in the trial, even though he was in such a state that she was actually frightened of him. In my opinion, that did not demonstrate the best level of patient care. She was shocked that the verdict was guilty. That is not usually the reaction of a prosecution witness. The prosecution had won the case. She was their witness, she was batting on their side but she was shocked that they had won. If she was so sure Cole was guilty of manslaughter, not murder, why did she not give evidence for the defence, I wondered? So this woman gave evidence for the prosecution, allowed her patient to give evidence while he was (as she said in the affidavit) in no fit state and then made a fuss when the case was proved. I went over the information in my mind and wondered at the sort of muddled thinking this demonstrated.

The families of the victims of the horrific murders had now had a second trial to go through. The trauma that is caused to families of murder victims during a trial is common knowledge and has been for many years. It is a dreadful experience. Dr Foy was instrumental in putting two families through a second helping of that sort of trauma. That, to my mind, demonstrated very little in the way of empathy.

Doctors had been responsible for the illegal removal of the records from the Trust. Nobody had been prosecuted. I wondered at the morality of people who would purposefully remove evidence before a murder trial. I had formed a very low opinion of them; my opinion was that they were amoral, devious and uncaring. I reminded myself what they did for a living. Ah, yes. They made decisions about the mental processes of other people and made decisions about how they should be treated. Exactly who, I wondered, was in charge of the asylum.

No wonder Wendy had developed a mistrust of doctors.

CHAPTER 17

Tea and Transcripts

Over the coming weekend, I settled down to read Wendy's paperwork. I spent hours with the transcript of the second trial.

Medical records, or notes, were provided at that trial. These gave details of the family background of the Coles. I was able to piece together a picture of Andrew Cole's life. He was born on 11 June 1969. The family lived in a flat above their shoe shop in the High Street in Presteigne. During his early years, Cole would go to his grandmother if he was disciplined by his mother and she would 'cuddle it away' and take him off to her house.

When he was told that his mother was expecting another baby, he began to act strangely. He would not touch his mother and said that she had fleas. If she touched a door handle, he would wipe it clean. If she touched a cup, he would smash it. If she prepared Sunday lunch, he would insist that he was served first, before other members of the family. Eventually he would not eat any food prepared by her or let her wash any of his clothes. He would only eat food prepared by his grandmother.

He was jealous of his sister, Lisa and occasionally showed aggression towards her. He would be unpleasant to his grandmother and then ask for money for things like a computer. His mother wondered why he refused to accept food prepared by her but that he would accept money that she offered to him. He showed aggression to his mother and was verbally abusive. He would do nothing for the family without payment. He had no known problems at school and did well outside of the home environment.

He enjoyed attending the army cadets and joined the army in September 1985. He had a problem with an injury to his knee and came home that Christmas. He also had injuries to his face but made no explanation for these. He did not want to go back to the army and signed himself out. His attitude to his mother had not changed and he would not allow her to prepare his food or wash his clothes. He did not want to go out and could not, therefore, get a job or sign on as unemployed, so his family supported him financially. He spent his time reading books, especially outdoor books, playing his guitar and making clothes. His mother spoke to him through the door or would leave letters for him.

The following August, the family moved out of the flat, to go and live in a bungalow. None of them suggested that Andrew Cole move with them, they left him to live in the flat alone. He covered the windows with bedspreads because he did not want the neighbours looking in. He only went out at night or would go further afield during the day but would not go out locally during the day. He also went on two family holidays, to Cornwall and to Ireland.

He gave an explanation for locking himself away, when he was in Talgarth Hospital. He said that, when he was sixteen, he went to a dance in Knighton. He got drunk on lager and cider. A girl called Claire hit him across his forehead. He denied that he punched her. He said that there were witnesses. He was worried that her brother would take revenge on him and claimed that everyone accused him and made slanderous comments about him.

He and the rest of the family received abundant medical attention. When he was four years old, Cole was taken to see a Dr Schofield, who noted that he was boisterous, hyperactive and always wanted his Nan if disciplined by Mr or Mrs Cole. In 1979, the health visitor noticed that Cole was reacting to the new baby and he was referred on. He saw Dr Floren, a psychotherapist, Dr Dawe, a child psychiatrist and Dr Newberry, an educational psychologist. Dr Dawe wrote to Cole's GP and said that there was a staggering abnormal behaviour in all parties.

In 1983, a chartered clinical psychologist, Dr Wilkinson became involved with the Cole family when the case was referred to him from their GP. He organized family therapy sessions and diagnosed 'manipulative behaviour'. On 7 September 1983, he had written in his notes that Mr Cole had a temper, Mrs Cole was crazy and Andrew Cole a naughty boy whose father and grandmother allow normal childhood things to get out of hand. When examined by Lord Thomas about this record, Dr Wilkinson had claimed that would have been said to try and get the family to start talking. Lord Thomas asked him if that meant he had told the family something which was untrue in order to try and get them to talk. He agreed that he had. I wondered how he interpreted the word 'manipulative' when he had made his diagnosis - did he consider that telling a lie in order to get someone to comply with your wishes was manipulative behaviour? If so, he wasn't above using that sort of behaviour himself.

This was the not only example of the medical professionals explaining that they had lied. Mrs Cole was a patient of Dr Foy. Mrs Cole explained what was happening at home and asked for help in dealing with Andrew Cole. A warrant was applied for and granted. Dr Foy went to Cole's flat with a social worker, a nurse and the police. Cole was forcibly removed and taken to Talgarth Hospital in handcuffs.

Dr Foy wrote a report that stated the reasons for his admission. She said that she was of the opinion that Andrew Cole was suffering from a mental disorder, which warrants hospital treatment and that this was in the interest of his safety and that of the public. She went on to say that Cole had a complete lack of insight that he was ill, refused any interventions, appeared acutely paranoid and 'is a danger to himself and others'. When Dr Hessian, who was giving evidence for the prosecution, was questioned about this, his response was that he believed she would have written this to provide for 'sectioning' under the Mental Health Act which is the process by which people are made to go to hospital as patients. She had only known Andrew Cole a couple of hours.

There are legal requirements regarding carting people off and locking them up under the Mental Health Act. The law says that you must have a good reason for this. The (now retired) consultant psychiatrist of Talgarth informed the court that a report describing the mental health of a person who had been detained under this Act had been a fiction, to cover the requirements of the law. Dr Foy had not seen Cole before he (Cole) was removed from his flat. She took action based on information given to her by one of her patients. In order to obtain the warrant, a social worker would have had to swear on oath that Cole was either being ill-treated or neglected, or that he was unable to care for himself and 'carry on in such a place'. In her evidence, Dr Foy said that Andrew Cole was brought out of his flat looking dirty and frightened. When he arrived at the hospital, notes were taken by someone called Tom Harvey. These recorded the facts that the handcuffs were removed and that Cole appeared clean and frightened. It is unlikely that Cole were washed on his way to the hospital in handcuffs. If he was dirty, this would indicate that he was not looking after himself very well. It is therefore feasible that Dr Foy was saying that he was dirty to support her actions. Two doctors were required to recommend sectioning, so Dr Harvey was instructed and saw Cole the following day. It was not clear from the papers whether this was the same person as Tom Harvey who made the earlier notes or someone else entirely.

There were more legal qualifications in that courtroom than you could shake a stick at, but nobody uttered the words 'wrongful arrest' or 'false imprisonment' so perhaps it is accepted practice that doctors may make formal, convenient but essentially incorrect statements in order to enable people to be removed to and detained in hospital. It was all a bit worrying. Instead of saying to Mrs Cole, 'Well stop leaving food and drink outside his door and he'll come out when he's hungry,' like most of us would have done, medical professionals had confirmed that Cole was unable to care for himself and was a danger to himself or others, called the police and had him detained in hospital.

I looked at some of the advice given to the Cole family by the many professionals who had dealings with them. When Andrew Cole was young, social services had suggested that he go and live with his grandmother, Mrs Martin. Dr Newberry had discussed Mrs Cole giving up the shop. Dr Dawe had advised that Cole needed psychotherapy. Dr Wilkinson had thought that the purchase of the bungalow was a good idea, but it had taken years before this had been achieved and he believed this was another matter that would not be seen through.

●　　●　　●

I wondered how I would have coped if one of my children had demanded to be served first when I was putting out the Sunday dinner. What would I have done if one of them had refused to eat food that I had prepared? If one of them had refused to wear clothes that had been washed by me, how would I have responded? It didn't take a lot of thinking about. I would have served them last. I would have given them their food myself. If they had refused to eat it, I would have let them wait for the next meal and given them food again. I would wash their clothes and leave them in their pyjamas if they wouldn't get dressed.

Children can be difficult. They are most unlikely, though, to starve themselves to a state of malnourishment, simply because they can't have their own way. They are unlikely to go to school in pyjamas just to annoy you, at least not more than once. Most adults have an advantage over their children. They are usually able to outwit them. Andrew Cole's family, with their huge team of professionals, appeared helpless in the face of an eight year old with a bad temper.

● ● ●

By the time Cole was sixteen and had returned from his four-month army career, they were unable to retrieve the situation and escaped from him by moving into the bungalow and leaving him in the flat. When he decided that he wouldn't go out, they provided for all his needs. He never worked or claimed benefits. He managed to get himself out of the flat when they invited him on holiday, though. I imagined his mother, standing close to his door and talking to him, begging him to come out. She seemed unable to work out why he resented her so much. I could guess. When you are a child, you need someone to look after you because the world is a big place and there are lots of things that you don't understand and things that scare you. You need to rely on someone who can deal with all those things that are out there. That makes you feel secure and safe. You test the people who are looking after you, just to make sure they are big enough and strong enough and wise enough to guide you through the world and its mysterious ways. Andrew Cole must have been terribly disappointed to discover that he was stronger and smarter than his own parents.

Dr Hessian said that Andrew Cole's problems had been caused as a result of women. I don't agree. I think problems were caused by the fact that the women were totally disempowered by the professionals they came into contact with. These professionals had been clever enough to note the power struggle between each and every member of the Cole family. They had, however, quite overlooked the fact that they too had entered the arena and were merely confirming that the family group was failing. They dished out interventions, recommendations and referrals. They were clever and used long words. Faced with a host of qualified professionals and their educated recommendations and diagnoses, the Cole family must have felt quite inadequate to deal with the problems in their home.

I could find nothing in the transcript to suggest that the family had been encouraged to take control of the child themselves. The disrespectful comments such as 'staggering abnormal behaviour in all parties' and 'Mrs Cole is crazy' that the professionals either added to notes or wrote to each other, testified that the professionals deemed the family incapable. The problems created by the child were represented to the family as complex and quite beyond their aptitude.

Andrew Cole, meanwhile, was growing bigger and stronger in a home environment where people acquiesced to his will.

CHAPTER 18

Stress

Andrew Cole's handcuffs were removed and he settled down to a few weeks as an in-patient in Talgarth. He explained his lifestyle by telling the story of the girl at the dance in Knighton, in great detail. This was recorded as obsessional paranoia. I would like to hear from Claire, the young woman who Cole had accused of hitting him and as the reason for his hiding at home during the day-time, back in 1996. Did she hit Cole across the forehead and then falsely accuse him of punching her? Perhaps that was not the truth. Perhaps Cole had assaulted her and her brother really was looking for revenge. That could explain why he went into hiding. When does a person come out of hiding? Like the Japanese soldier who spent twenty years or so guarding a small island because nobody told him the war was over, how do you know when it's time to come out?

One of the main reasons for instigating a compulsory admission to hospital under the Mental Health Act is to carry out an assessment. It says so, right there in the Act under 'admission for assessment'. Dr Foy asked Dr Wilkinson to carry out the assessment. Dr Wilkinson saw Andrew Cole twice. The first time he saw Cole, he went through a questionnaire with him, called a DSSI, which stands for Delusion, Signs and Symptoms Inventory. It is a list of symptoms and the doctor ticks the 'true' box if the patient confirms that he or she suffers from the symptom and the 'false' box if they don't. There are about eighty-four questions on the form. Andrew Cole only answered 'true' to two symptoms, even though Dr Wilkinson believed he should have answered 'true' to many more.

The second time Dr Wilkinson saw him, he handed him an MMPR test (a multiple choice questionnaire) to complete. Despite requests, Cole never completed the form. Dr Wilkinson was therefore unable to carry out the assessment. I wondered if Dr. Wilkinson had stood at the other side of the door and begged Cole to come out and hand him the completed questionnaire. Like Mrs. Cole, he was helpless in the face of Cole's refusal to co-operate.

After Cole committed the murders, Dr Wilkinson prepared a report. I hope he mentioned doors, and shutting them after horses have bolted.

One entry in Cole's medical records from Talgarth, which I spotted on the transcript, has given me a money saving idea. The entry, dated December 31 said 'AC was seen by a locum (not qualified, wife of GP). ' This is useful! It costs so much, nowadays to have gas appliances checked by qualified professionals. Perhaps we can all write little notes that say, 'Tested on such-and-such-a-date, not by a CORGI registered plumber, but she is married to one and knows ever such a lot about it.' That should do it -we can save ourselves a small fortune.

Dr Foy took the stand as a defence witness on the second occasion. At least, I thought, she knew whose side she was batting on this time. I expected that she had a tremendous insight to offer the court. Her evidence was the reason for holding a second trial, after all. This is what she had to say: 'At his first trial I saw him coping less and less and thought he'd crack under the stress. When I visited him in the cells, I saw a different person – violent, wild, aggressive and terrifying. I felt this change was due to the stress of listening all through the doctor's evidence. I concluded he had been suffering from a severe personality disorder all along.' She said a little more, of course, but that is the crux of the new evidence that she presented to the court.

That little gem, I thought, ensured that the previous sentence was quashed and two bereaved families went through a second trial. That stunning piece of mental agility gave Christopher the opportunity to insist that he be allowed to attend court. He had not been allowed to attend the first trial but he argued that he should be present for the re-trial. After all, he was older and he needed to know what was being said about his brother. Christopher won the argument and attended. Lord Thomas didn't notice Christopher, behind him. He held up a photograph of William. He told Cole that he had better not show him the photograph because he remembered how upset he got when he saw it before. He held it up so that Cole could see the plain back of the photograph. Christopher saw the face of his dead brother, his expression frozen in horror above an open, gaping wound that had once been his throat. Time, for Christopher, stopped at that moment. Wendy tried to pull him away, but Christopher was as unmoveable as the statue he had become. Sergeant Price moved quickly to throw his body between the photograph and the boy but it was too late. Time had stopped for Christopher and he saw nothing but the expression on the face of his dead brother for an endless, endless moment.

Wendy knows that part of Christopher is still standing there, rooted to the spot. The rest of him went out and got stoned. He broke into cars and moved them about so that people got up the next morning and wondered why their car was across the road and their neighbour's car was outside their house. Christopher thought it was funny. Christopher was full of pranks. He laughed when he went to prison and played some more pranks when he came back out. He needed to be taught a lesson, so he went to prison again. He laughed and laughed and it was ten long years full of punishments before anybody saw the post-traumatic stress that he hid inside in that place where he stood in front of the photograph and wondered why he couldn't cry.

It was not the first time that Andrew Cole had been that different person. William and Fiona saw that different person. He was violent, wild, aggressive and terrifying. He was stabbing them over and over and over again.

Perhaps, I thought, Dr. Foy could have taken into consideration that standing trial for the murder of two people is a stressful situation. It should not have surprised her that Cole found it an ordeal. He wasn't used to criticism. He was used to getting his own way. Suddenly he was in the dock with the prospect of a mandatory life sentence hanging over him. There was a room full of people listening to him try and explain why he had stabbed two people to death. He was obviously not enjoying himself. He was showing signs of stress. I hope she realises now that certain situations cause people to feel stress, taking part in a penalty shoot-out for your national side, being a crew member in a space shuttle, going out on patrol in Iraq, telling someone their child has been murdered. Life is not always easy. People get stressed. They may react by screaming or crying. It doesn't mean they have a personality disorder.

Once again, evidence was given to the effect that, after slaughtering his victims, Andrew Cole went to the hospital in Llandod. The nurses cleaned him up and took a clump of hair out his clenched, right fist. Dr Hilsden wrote a report to say that he had gone to the bungalow. He saw a naked body - a young male with short fair hair was face down on the floor. There was blood around the body. There were no visible wounds, no signs of life. Life was pronounced extinct.

There were twelve stab wounds to William's back, ranging in size from ten centimetres to two centimetres. There were two stab wounds to his left buttock and another two on the junction between the neck and the back. Of the forty stab wounds that had been inflicted on William, sixteen would be visible while he was lying on his front. Dr Hilsden's statement was read out to the court during the second trial. It was not questioned.

A decision was reached based largely on psychiatric evidence. Was Cole responsible for his behaviour? Was the provocation such as to make a reasonable person act in the way that Cole had acted?

•   •   •

The jury considered all the evidence and found Andrew Cole guilty of murder for the second time. Dr Foy must have been furious. She told the jury that she had changed her mind and decided that Andrew Cole had a severe personality disorder all along but they still hadn't listened to her. For the second time, Andrew Cole heard the words 'Take him down.'

CHAPTER 19

An Ovation For Wendy

Wendy still wanted to know more. She was still being starved of facts. She wanted to know if Cole should or should not have been discharged from Talgarth Hospital. It wasn't enough that two juries had decided that he was responsible for his behaviour, they may not have had all the facts. They may not have understood all the facts. She needed to hear from the staff at Talgarth.

• • •

A bundle of letters recorded the battle that Wendy, the Community Health Council of Wales and the Zito Trust fought with Powys Health Trust. The Zito Trust that was set up in 1994 by Jayne Zito and Michael Howlett, following the murder of Jonathan Zito and offers support and advice to victims of mentally disordered offenders, particularly secondary victims of homicide.

Wendy had been so innocent at first, so trusting. She thought that she could ask them to talk to her and, out of a sense of moral obligation and compassion, they would.

Jane Jeffs wrote the first letter, asking for a meeting between the doctors involved, herself, Wendy and Brian. Not only did they not want to talk to her, it seemed that there was no credible internal inquiry taking place. Eventually the Zito Trust became involved when Wendy and Jane turned to them for help. The request for information became a demand, the demand became a battle.

Eventually · a meeting was arranged with a view to undertaking an Independent Review. Wendy agreed to this because it seemed that was all that was on offer. Dr Hessian and Dr Foy chose not to attend the meeting and not to contribute anything to the investigation that the Health Care Trust attempted. They would reveal nothing and thwarted any attempt to uncover facts about the care they had offered and the decisions they had made.

Eventually Wendy called in the Ombudsman. She had to put together a complaint and state a clear case for the Ombudsman to investigate. She wanted to know if the staff had been remiss in their decision to allow Andrew Cole to walk out of that hospital without a proper package of continuing care. She was concerned at the apparent failings within the hospital and the attitude of the doctors.

The Ombudsman agreed to conduct an investigation. I met Wendy five years after the murders, but I arrived in her life before the Ombudsman's report. The report documents how Dr Hessian removed the medical notes and refused to give them back, even when threatened with legal action. He argued that the paper was his and the intellectual content was his, so he would not hand them over. Dr Hessian and Dr Foy declined to co-operate with enquires made by the Health Trust. Under no circumstances would they meet with Wendy. Dr Hessian even challenged, by means of a judicial review in the High Court, the right of the Ombudsman to investigate the complaint. This challenge was unsuccessful. They battled on. Eventually, on 17 October 2002 the Ombudsman's report concluded that Andrew Cole was discharged appropriately. It did uphold the complaint that the matter had not been appropriately investigated and recommended that the National Assembly of Wales should devise and promulgate (I had to look that word up, it means to put a something into effect by formal public announcement) a clear policy regarding the investigation of serious incidents such as this one and the establishment of inquiries under section 84 of the National Health Service Act 1977 (this gives more powers to the person holding the inquiry).

The battle that Wendy had embarked upon, with the support of Jane Jeffs and Michael Howlett of the Zito Trust, had resulted in a policy being put into place that would change the way in which investigations of serious incidents such as the murders of William and Fiona would be conducted. It had taken five years. It had drained Wendy. The shock of discovering that people would not talk to her about the events leading up to the death of her son had damaged her and diminished her self-esteem. She had been determined that it should not happen to anybody else. Now, it would not.

Wendy had other questions to ask of doctors, though. There had been two trials, each one ending in a verdict of 'guilty'. The Ombudsman's report had concluded that Andrew Cole was appropriately discharged into the community. Andrew Cole was sane. Andrew Cole should have spent a very long time in prison. Andrew Cole did not. He had been removed to Broadmoor Special Hospital under section 47 and 49 of the Mental Health Act 1983 (section 49 is a restriction on the terms of his release) and is under in the care of a Health Authority instead. Two doctors would have been required to sign a statement to the fact that he was suffering from a mental illness. Wendy had doubts that Andrew Cole should have been released from Talgarth. She believed that, because he had been removed to Broadmoor, this suggested he was mentally ill. She believed that doctors may have hidden some evidence and covered up the fact that he should not have been discharged.

I had doubts that the decision to remove him to Broadmoor was a reliable one. I could see how easy it was to get two doctors to offer a written opinion and sign the relevant paperwork. Still, I understood where she was coming from. I wanted to let her get it off her chest.

Wendy attended one conference in London where she was down as the first speaker after lunch. During the lunch break she placed a piece of paper on every seat. When the audience returned, she took to the stage and introduced herself. She gave them background information and then said:

'Excuse me doctors
Could you look my way?
I'm stopping where I am
And I will not go away
I've got some questions
You could answer me today.
You know what happened
To my young man son.
Slashed a hundred slashes
Until his life was gone.
But did you know his mother
Still bleeds from every one?
And I'm not looking
To name or blame or shame.
And I know my life
Will never be the same.
And I know I'll never
See him smile his smile again.
But I know that you should tell me,
Don't let me ask in vain.
Answer all my questions,
Don't play this nasty game.
I just want to know
I need to understand
What happened to the man
That raised his killing hand?
Who let him out to slaughter?
Who didn't see his rage?
Who missed the smell of blood?
Who opened up his cage?
Excuse me doctors
Could you look my way?
I'm stopping where I am
And I will not go away.
I've got some questions
You should answer me today.'

Wendy had rehearsed. She could read it with passion and feeling. She stood proudly to receive her standing ovation. She noted that nobody left the poem on their seat when they left. It might not have changed the world but it made a lot of people think about things. They wanted to know about her experience. She answered the many questions that were put to her.

I had thrown my hat in with Wendy, championing better treatment and care for the families of murder and manslaughter. I wondered if this was why I had met her. I was eventually to discover that it was not.

CHAPTER 20

Flashbacks

I met a lot of legal professionals during my time as Witness Service Manager at Huddersfield Magistrates' Court. Legal advisors were a permanent fixture and my office was opposite theirs. I often asked for help in understanding the procedures, so that I could advise witnesses appropriately. I always received the help I sought and was grateful to work with such a decent bunch of people. Defence advocates were usually local solicitors and I became friendly with them during my time there. The Crown Prosecution Service often used agents to prosecute cases. I became particularly fond of some of them.

One agent was Barbara. I liked her immediately. She was about my age and her intelligence was not intimidating. There was something approachable, friendly and kind about Barbara.

One day Barbara came in to speak to a prosecution witness who was waiting to give evidence. 'Are you nervous?' she kindly asked the witness, who was visibly shaking. 'Terrified,' she answered. 'Just try this,' said Barbara and showed the witness how to do a sequence of taps, mostly on her face and hand. The witness copied what Barbara was doing. I had never seen anything like it and wondered what on earth she was up to. 'Does that feel better?' asked Barbara when the taps had been completed. The witness looked astounded. 'Yes, it does!' she declared.

Later I asked Barbara what she had been doing and she explained that it was a new treatment, which works on the mind and body system, based on a mixture of modern understanding of brain function and the ancient understanding of energy meridians. It could be used to treat anxiety and was sometimes used by therapists to treat post-traumatic stress. I said that this could be an excellent tool for the Court Witness Service and asked her if she could teach me. Barbara did better than that. She offered to put on a training session, about post traumatic stress, for free. I decided to share this across West Yorkshire and invited other managers to come to the training session so that they could take it back to their courts and teach their volunteers.

The training session was designed to provide Witness Service teams with an understanding of post-traumatic stress and to give them a non-threatening self-help technique, which they could then share with witnesses to alleviate their anxiety - and did not involve the witness being required to talk about the stressful events. At the training session, we explored with Barbara the physical and mental effects of post-traumatic stress. She then allowed us to try a tapping sequence for ourselves. She first warned us not to revisit any memories that were stressful or traumatic because it would not be appropriate to deal with those in a workshop. Rather, we should think about something that had caused us some lesser degree of anxiety or stress and then go through a sequence of taps on our face and hands. I couldn't think of anything so I just tapped and it had no effect. One member of the group had a different experience. There was something that had bothered her immensely and the tapping had brought an instant relief. We went out to lunch together and she gave Barbara a big hug, telling her that she couldn't thank her enough.

I was intrigued but crippled by the scepticism that has prevented me from believing in anything that I can't see, hear or otherwise sense. Barbara explained to me that she was a sceptic too but had come to accept that this could be effective because she had seen it work. She also explained that the tapping sequences should not always be expected to be effective. No therapeutic approach can ever be *guaranteed* to work. If anyone has acute anxiety or post traumatic stress, she explained, their doctor may prescribe medication or refer the person for specialist treatment with one of several available forms of psychotherapeutic help.

●　　　●　　　●

I went home and thought about post-traumatic stress and Wendy. I didn't know what to say to her. I didn't know if it worked or if I could deal with it like Barbara had. I practised on my youngest son, Andrew for days. He didn't have any trauma that he could think of and it did nothing to him, but it gave me the chance to go over the routine again and again so that I got it right.

When I believed I had mastered it, I 'phoned Wendy. I explained that I didn't really know what I was doing and it might not work but did she want to give it a go? She did. I went over that evening, after one last practice session with Andrew.

I sat next to Wendy-Lou on the sofa and then asked Wendy if there was anything that came back to her in the form of flashbacks. Of course there was. I asked her to think of one such thing and give it a mark out of ten. Ten was the greatest pain and nought was no pain. She looked at me as though I was daft and said that, of course, it was a ten. I taught the routine to her and then asked her to think about the traumatic image while she went through the routine, with me talking her through it so she didn't have to think about the routine, only the traumatic image. She became hot and breathless during the routine. When we had completed it, I told her to relax and then think about it again and give it another score. She frowned in a moment of uncertainty and gave it a score of seven. We repeated the exercise and she was able to give it a score of three. We went through the routine once more and then I asked her to give it a score again. She was silent for a moment.

She looked at me as though I were a demon and said 'WHAT have YOU done to ME?' She got up and walked toward the door, announcing, 'I'm going to the bathroom.'

Neither Wendy Lou nor I moved or spoke. What had I done to her? I didn't know. I was messing about with something I didn't understand. I daren't move a muscle. We heard Wendy coming back down the stairs and then she entered the room. 'I have been the toilet' she announced 'and I shut the bathroom door after myself.' I sat there like a ventriloquist's dummy, only moving my eyes. 'It was the mortuary' she explained. 'That moment when I saw William and heard the door closing behind me. I haven't been able to close a door behind me for years. When I go to a public toilet, I have to get Wendy Lou to stand outside so that I can leave the door ajar. I've just closed the door.'

'That's good, then, is it?' I eventually managed to ask.

'Good? No, it's not good. It's amazing!' she declared.

I was beginning to stop fearing for my safety. I asked her if she would like to work on any other flashbacks. She did and we repeated the exercise twice more with exactly the same results.

Wendy explained that these images had come into her mind every day, many times a day, every time she heard certain noises or doors closed or any number of other things that could trigger them. Each time an image came into her head she would feel a rush of physical pain that started at the pit of her stomach and engulfed her body. She had lived like this for years, being washed over with pain many times every day.

She felt better. She was amazed and astounded. She thanked me as I left, many times. I was feeling deeply sceptical and left with a bag of worries in my hand. It was, I believed, a flash in the pan. It was some strange little psychosomatic effect that had fooled us. I was convinced that she would wake up the following morning and be exactly as she had been the morning before. She would feel terribly disappointed and let down.

I went to work the next morning and thought about her most of the day. When I got home I rang her number. A strange voice answered the phone. I didn't recognise it. I asked for Wendy and the voice laughed. It was Wendy. Gone was the flat monotone that could create a little cloud above my head when I was speaking to her. In its place was a rich voice with tones and rhythm.

'I've got brown eyes,' she said, for no particular reason that I could think of.

'Yes, I know. You've got hazel-brown eyes,' I replied.

'No, no. I had light eyes. They have been a light colour ever since William was murdered. I got up this morning and looked in the mirror and I could see myself in there. I had my own eyes back, brown eyes. I could see they were a darker shade than before. They were back to normal. I recognised myself. I could see it was me, Wendy. I haven't looked like Wendy for a long, long time.'

There were other miraculous benefits. Wendy could now think about William. She could remember him as a small boy, picture him growing up. The pain had prevented her from visiting any happy memories for years. Now she had access to them. She could enjoy some of those memories.

This was not a cure. She still had a lot of problems. She didn't sleep well. She still felt angry about a lot of things and she still felt sad. It did, however take away the torturous pain that had crippled her every day for years. It was one step towards an acceptable quality of life. It was a permanent step. Some of the load that Wendy carried had been lifted. She felt lighter, happier.

Wendy's company became more enjoyable as she carried less of her load. We laughed more than ever. We talked about a whole range of things that we had never previously explored. I wanted Jo to see the transformation, she would be surprised.

●　　●　　●

When Jo came up for the weekend we went out to Hebden Bridge for the day. The sun shone on us. We went into a lovely restaurant for lunch and sat at an outside table by the river. We poked around in all the little shops. I bought a quarter of marzipan teacakes because there is a shop there that sells them and is, as far as I know, the last place on earth where you can get marzipan teacakes. They remind me of my childhood. They remind me of my dad. Each of us spotted some sweeties that reminded us of something in our distant past. It is more than a sweet shop, it is the place to go to buy a taste of one's childhood.

Jo was appropriately surprised and delighted at the change in Wendy. She was astounded at the physical change in her appearance. Wendy walked in a different way, moved in a different way, stood taller. We no longer had a relationship with Wendy and her trauma. We had a relationship with Wendy. She was better without it.

This is, I believe, worth thinking about. A person who is in a state of torment is less fun than a person who isn't. The consequences are that they become isolated. Many people will find them hard work as company. They lose their friends. Life becomes less and less bearable for them. This is how we deal with innocent victims.

A final word in this chapter must go to Barbara. Wendy, her family and her friends thank you for your kindness, your selflessness and your guidance. Thank you, Barbara, for your gift.

CHAPTER 21

Conferences and Challenges

Wendy was looking forward to speaking at a conference in Birmingham. It was another conference that had been arranged in order for there to be consultation between the families of victims of murder and manslaughter and professionals of the agencies within the Criminal Justice System. Wendy was proud to have been invited to speak. She was going to use the recent victim impact statement that we had created, as the basis of her presentation. The victim impact statement had been requested because Andrew Cole was expecting yet another court appearance. After the second trial, he had been given a mandatory life sentence and the judge had recommended that he serve no less than fifteen years before he could be considered by the Parole Board for release. As was the procedure with such cases, this recommendation had gone before a High Court judge. This judge had looked at all the paperwork and noted that the judge in the first trial had, as he wrote in a letter to the Lord Chief Justice, concluded that he was astounded the jury had found the defendant guilty of murder, rather than manslaughter. Because of this, the High Court judge recommended to the Home Secretary that Cole should serve no less than eleven years before he was considered for release. (This system of setting a tariff was changed in recent years due to the effects of the Human Rights Act.)

Eleven years was a derisory sentence for a killer who had been found guilty of the murder of two people. Wendy and Jane wrote a pile of letters and eventually managed to persuade the Home Secretary to impose a fifteen year tariff on Cole. It seemed most unfair that the High Court judge had taken into consideration the words of the judge in the first trial. After all, this trial had been quashed in order to let Cole be re-tried. By referring to that transcript, the High Court judge had allowed Cole to have his cake and eat it – to maintain the benefits of the first trial but also a second chance to have his defence presented. Cole had been given the best of both worlds.

Legal arguments have resulted in the conclusion that the Home Secretary may no longer over-ride decisions made in court and, as I write this, all offenders with tariffs set by the Home Secretary are having their cases considered in the courts. Most will have their sentences reduced. None may have their sentences increased. The impact statement will be read by the judge who is considering Cole's case. It is almost ten years since his trial. He could be released very soon. Wendy and her family are not ready to face that just yet. I worded the impact statement for her applying great consideration to that task. I hope it hits home.

Is it fair that the impact statement is written by someone other than the victim? The offender has a barrister to speak for them. The barrister has been trained to speak in court and present his or her client's case with impact. Should victims be tied up in a corner and gagged, just in case they say something that throws a spanner in the works? No, I'd like to get someone like Seamus Heaney to write the impact statement. He can do things with words that make me cry my eyes out. One line of a poem, written by this man, might haunt me for decades. I wished that he could write Wendy's impact statement so that the judge broke down, weeping uncontrollably and went home with the words sitting inside his head, humming a quiet lament to keep him awake at nights. The one I wrote won't be able to do that, but I tried my best!

Howard Webber, the chief executive of the Criminal Injuries Compensation Authority had been a speaker at the Birmingham conference. Wendy trapped him in a web like a spider traps a fly.

As mentioned in an earlier chapter, after William was murdered, the social security had given Wendy a loan to pay for William's funeral. They refused to give her a grant because they said that she would receive a payout from the CICA in due course. She had duly applied for a grant for funeral expenses from them, but the application had been refused. The refusal explained that 'Because of William's criminal convictions and lifestyle, he may have contributed to his own death.'

William was eighteen years old. He had a string of minor convictions, none of which involved violence. He had attended rehab in order to turn his life around. He had no alcohol or drugs in his system when he was brutally stabbed to death. In what way did these people think William had contributed to his own death? What it appeared they were saying was, 'William deserved it.'

Out of anger that this could be implied, rather than a desire for the money, Wendy put in an appeal. She attended an oral hearing in Cardiff. In the waiting room was a police officer who had been called to give evidence against William. There were three men, with their suitcases at the ready beside them, in the room. Wendy and her solicitor went before them and they told her that William had cost society enough already. The chairman actually started totting up how much William had cost, in pounds. Nick, the solicitor, tried to explain how well William had been doing in the six months before he was murdered but he was interrupted by the chairman, who said, 'Well, he was still on probation, wasn't he?' The chairman then said, with sarcasm, 'I wish that we could help you but it is impossible to make any award or even reimburse you for the funeral. Do we really want to endure putting the police officer on the stand to give evidence?' Nick was squashed, 'No, sir' he replied.

'Appeal dismissed!' announced the chairman.

Wendy was humiliated and degraded. She walked down the stairs, thinking how William was viewed as a burden to a society that would not grieve for him.

As she walked down the stairs, the three panel members came hurtling down and rushed past them on the stairs, then ran across the road to the railway station.

I hope they missed their train. I hope they missed that one and that the next was cancelled and they had to change somewhere that nobody has ever heard of and wait another few hours and then be misdirected onto the wrong train. I hope it was the worst possible train journey that anyone could ever embark upon.

At the conference, Howard Webber gave a presentation about how the CICA came to its decisions and what they pay, how long it takes and why. He said 'All the families of murder and manslaughter victims are reimbursed for the funeral costs.' From the floor, Wendy said, 'All families are not.' He replied 'Yes, they are' and continued with his presentation.

Wendy stored up that little exchange and took to the stage. She gave her presentation as planned about the impact statement and what victims mean when they say that they have to live a 'life sentence' that truly means life. She continued with an unscripted piece of information, she explained that part of that life sentence is actually imposed upon the families by the failings of society and gave her dealings with the CICA as an example. She aimed her gaze at the face of Howard Webber, who was sitting in the front row. He spoke up, 'That's not right. There is no way that happened. I can assure you that all victims' families are reimbursed for funeral costs.'

Wendy gazed down at him. She was feeling calm and strong. 'Are you suggesting that this did not happen? I can assure you that it did.' She was speaking in the sort of voice that suggests that she might be about to hurt somebody.

A voice called out from the auditorium, 'She's right. I didn't get it either.' Then another. 'I didn't get it.'

Someone shouted, 'Hands up all those who didn't get it.'

Hands went up, many hands. Howard Webber looked horrified.

They spoke late that evening, Wendy and Howard Webber. He said that he would look into the matter. It was not very many weeks before he let her know that it was over six years since she put in for the appeal. It was too late for him to do anything about it.

Wendy didn't care about the money. She never has. She calls it blood money and points out that it is her son's blood she is referring to.

I think people ought to know, though. This is who the CICA are and this is what we taxpayers pay them to do.

Within a month she was due to speak at another conference and this one was especially important to her. It is an annual conference, hosted by NEVA. NEVA is the North of England Victims Association and is chaired by a dear friend of Wendy's, David Hines. Every year they hold a conference, at no cost to over one hundred families of the victims of murder and manslaughter. It takes place over one weekend and is a chance for these families to get together. They also invite outside speakers and professionals in order to explore issues and exchange information.

Wendy was looking forward to catching up with many old friends at the conference. They understand each other. They feel comfortable in each other's company. Pain has bound them together whilst all other bonds with society have frayed. I was often taken aback when I chatted with Wendy. We all talk about the people in our lives. Our companion sometimes needs reminding who is who, when we are telling our tale. 'You know, Anne, my cousin,' I might say, or 'No, not that Mary, the Mary I know from work.' Not Wendy. Wendy would say, 'You know who I mean, the one whose sister was killed by Fred West' or 'You remember, her son's body was never found.' I knew that I didn't want my life peopled in this way. They may be lovely people but I preferred the bonds of friendship to be free of a shared trauma.

She was also looking forward to walking on the beach, getting away for a couple of days and hearing the presentations. I hoped that everybody would see how much better she was looking. I hoped she now had the capacity to gain more enjoyment from the weekend than she had done before.

She was full of it when she came back. The weather had been good. She'd seen everybody and yes, they noticed how well she was looking. It was good to see her gaining health and strength as that year progressed. Life, for Wendy and her family, never will be the same again. Wendy will never be completely whole, completely well. She was, however making progress toward an acceptable quality of life and this is the best she can hope for.

It is also worth noting that NEVA struggle for funding to continue to host these events that are an important item in the calendar of the many family members of victims of murder and manslaughter. It is where they exchange information with professionals, where they bring to light problems that have been experienced as they make their way through a system that so often ignores them. These experiences can be taken back to the various agencies and the information used to improve the way in which these families are dealt with. Most of all, it is somewhere that the family members of victims can get together and feel accepted. They go somewhere for one whole weekend and feel as though they belong, somewhere where they don't feel isolated from everybody else.

I hope I never need NEVA but I would like to think that it continues to exist in order to offer all this for all the people who are going to become the relatives of murder or manslaughter victims this year, next year - and the year after that.

CHAPTER 22

Colours in the Garden

For the last eight years or so, Wendy has campaigned for some help to be put into place that can be offered to the families of victims of murder and manslaughter. It would be a package of care and involve a multi-agency partnership agreement. Nobody would impose help on these families. Help would be on offer. She would like a beautiful building that families can escape to, when they need to get away. She would like someone to recognise their needs. How do you cope when you are going through the aftermath of an event like this? Who helps children to cope with trauma when their parent or parents are so traumatised that they are struggling to cope themselves? Who reminds you that you still need to go shopping and pay the electricity bill when your world has just fallen apart? If the murder is not a high profile case, taking a front seat on every newspaper, you may have very little help.

She calls the building she dreams of a Respite Centre and has, on many occasions and to varied audiences, voiced the opinion that one should be set up. She has tried to source funding to set one up herself, but to no avail.

Wendy was delighted when she received a letter, inviting her to such a retreat. It was set up for the families of murder and manslaughter victims. This was a pilot project, and was called Escaping Victimhood. Another invitee on to this project was Margaret, who Wendy had known for several years. Margaret and her husband Tommy lived in Manchester, so Wendy arranged to meet Margaret so that they could travel together down to Beaconsfield, where the project was being run.

Tommy saw them onto the train from Manchester and, as they made their way along the platform, Wendy noted again how Margaret walked in the same way that she did. They both walked in a heavy-footed way, with their heads bowed. Wendy became more familiar with the shoes that people were wearing than with their faces. She knew that if she could see their face, they could see hers and she had become ashamed of the pain that controlled her own features and revealed itself in her every expression.

They arrived in the early afternoon and felt honoured to discover that the event was being held in a beautiful old house, surrounded by delightful gardens. They were greeted warmly and identified at Reception only by their first names. Introductions to the other participants were also by first names only. It was reassuring that such considerations had been made. The beauty of the venue demonstrated that the participants had been deemed worthy of such accommodation and the fact that first names were used indicated that the participants were going to be able to reveal as much or as little of their distressing family histories as they wished.

After a delicious lunch the participants and facilitators gathered together and it was explained that much was on offer but nothing was compulsory. The workshops that were available over the next four days would include art and music therapy, different types of massages, aromatherapy and trauma counselling. The building, the grounds and surrounding woods were freely accessible for walking, talking and relaxation. It was all very reassuring and a little of the fear-of-the-unknown, that had permeated the meeting, was dissipated.

The rest of the afternoon was spent wandering in the garden, talking and getting to know each other, not as secondary victims but as people. Wendy could feel herself relaxing. The feeling of acceptance and understanding was wonderful.

After dinner, all of the nine participants and two of the facilitators decided to go for a walk and wandered around the area until after dark. Their way back to the venue took them through a field and everybody giggled nervously when they realised that the field was already occupied by cows that shuffled about and moo-ed at the disturbance. The group had bonded. It was a good feeling.

All the participants started to retire to their rooms for the night and Wendy was the last to remain in the room where they had been drinking their nightcaps. In another room, four of the facilitators were still sitting up and talking. One of them noticed Wendy and asked if she would like to join them. Wendy accepted the invitation and joined in the conversation, which eventually got on to the subject of her fight for justice and better treatment for the families of victims of murder and manslaughter. She told them about the battle with Hereford Hospital and found herself becoming visibly emotional when she was describing the victory. This was most unusual for Wendy, who guarded the revealing of her emotions with a will of iron. Wendy realised that she was unveiling something about herself because she felt relaxed, comfortable and accepted. She believed that she had arrived at a place where she could find herself. Wendy had been lost for a long time. The trauma counsellor, Jay, noticed the welling up of emotion and invited Wendy to go with her into another room for a cup of tea.

Wendy and Jay talked about William and the aftermath of the murder. Wendy described the terrible physical pain that she suffered all the time. She told Jay that she was sure this pain was real, it was not psychological and she did not believe that she was mentally ill. Jay agreed that she was not and explained about the effects of trauma on the human body. She asked Wendy a lot of questions. Wendy was able to describe the way she had felt that she was sitting behind thick glass, unable to reach out to people, including her own family and how she felt that she was invisible behind the glass. She described the panic attacks she suffered. Talking to Jay was like opening a cupboard that was overfull of papers. The door opened and everything spilled out.

Jay described coping strategies and taught Wendy how to hold herself and breathe when she had a panic attack. The impromptu session was extraordinarily effective and, when Wendy went to bed, she went straight to sleep and slept through the remainder of the night for the first time in many years.

•   •   •

The next morning, after breakfast, Wendy went out into the garden. She didn't want to go and join in with the therapies. She felt that something was happening and she needed to be alone. She sat on a bench in the garden and felt the sun, warmly stroking her face. Lifting her head to look into the light, she noticed something peculiar demanding attention to her left hand side. She turned to meet this object and found, there, amongst the monochrome world that was her existence, a single, small blue flower, aglow with colour. This object of vibrant colour was so incongruous in her world that she was afraid and looked away. Daring hardly to breathe, she looked back again to see if it was still there. To her utter amazement the little blue flower showed Wendy the green of its leaves. This was not the muddy green that she had seen at Castle Hill. This was a jewel-like green, sitting brightly next to a glowing flower. It was too much, she could look at it no longer and turned her head away, only to be greeted by roses of yellow, red and pink. There were hundreds of roses celebrating their existence among leaves of deep green. Tears welled into Wendy's eyes and she knew that she was not alone any more. She looked to the trees beyond and saw many different shades of green. She had forgotten that green was not a single colour but a way of describing a host of varying shades.

Wendy moved her head to look for the blue flower and found a garden that was vibrant with colour and light. The blue flower was in the company of others, proudly displaying their yellows, pinks and purples. Something had happened, something that she didn't understand. It was still a little frightening to be amongst such beauty. She went over to the blue flower and gently caressed it between her finger and thumb. She looked at her hand, thinking the colours would have wiped off, but her hand was the colour of living flesh. Her instinct was to lie down among the flowers but she worried that someone may see her and resisted the urge.

Only her concern that people may think she was insane prevented Wendy from raising her hands to the sky and screaming 'I can see.' When one of the facilitators, Barbara, saw Wendy she saw that she was in some difficulty but had no way of knowing that Wendy was suppressing the urge to scream, shout and roll in the garden. Barbara asked Wendy if she would like to have a massage and, when Wendy agreed, took her to Carol. Carol started by doing some reflexology on Wendy's feet but a terrible pain caused Wendy to groan and she clutched at her stomach. Tears rolled down her face and Carol suggested that Wendy may have trapped all her pain in her stomach. Carol comforted Wendy and moved on to a soothing Indian head massage, until Wendy relaxed and she left her to rest. Immediately, Wendy went to sleep. Waking some half-hour later she was greeted by the exotic smells of the massage oils and the colours of the walls, the furniture and the towels. She felt awake, alive. She wandered back outside. The trapped pain had gone. Her stomach was free of pain for the first time in years and she finally stood up straight.

By the time she travelled back home she was standing straight and looking people in their eyes. Tommy went to meet Margaret and Wendy from the train and was amazed to see two women walking towards him, heads up and smiling broadly.

•   •   •

I was delighted to hear this tale, so it came as quite a surprise when Wendy's expression changed and she pointed her finger at me.

'But YOU have something to explain yourself about. I thought you were supposed to be my friend,' she said.

'Eh?' I said, eloquent in my surprise. She went on to explain that Tommy and Margaret brought her home in the car. She couldn't wait to see her home again and told them all about her house. She said that they would have to come in and have a cup of tea and see how lovely it was. She was chatting about it all the way back. They pulled up outside and walked into the front room. Wendy was just about to say, 'Here we are then' when she saw it, her recently-decorated front room. 'Oh my God!', she squawked as she took it in. It was red. It was three different shades of red. They all clashed.

'Why didn't you tell me?', she demanded.

'I thought you knew. I thought you liked it,' I said when we'd finished laughing.

Wendy reminded me that she really had not been able to see colour. She often mentioned colour, but she knew for example that the flowers in the hearse were blue and primrose because someone told her that they were. Her own eyes hadn't told her what colour things were for years.

It wasn't long before Wendy redecorated. I sit in her room now, grateful that she can see. The room is tastefully decorated in neutral colours and looks about twice the size that it was when I first saw it. She had to get rid of the carpet but she kept the large, red furniture that now rests comfortably against the restrained background.

Wendy was asked to give feedback about her time at the centre. She gave them a glowing report. It gave her the chance to take another step towards an acceptable quality of life. It gave her back colour. It is not possible to put a value on colour. This was the greatest gift she had ever been given. She did, however, voice some reservations. It would not have been helpful in the first few weeks or even months after the murder. There is more help that should be put in place for such families. It should involve practical as well as emotional help.

Wendy dreams of running such a service. She would like the service to own a beautiful house that is big enough to accommodate the need. Events such as the one she benefited from would be hosted there. She would also enhance the service, using the building to offer families a different kind of respite in the early days, when they are in shock and need to escape from the press and the pressure of the nightmare that has come along to take over their lives. An outreach service that offered a multi-agency response to incidents of murder and manslaughter would be co-ordinated. Families would be offered help to deal with the early, dark days, the days that steal the colour from your head. The building would be used to host training events, to teach professionals how to deal with families after such a crime, for example educational professionals would be informed how children may respond to the murder or manslaughter of a relative, health services would be informed about the impact of health on such family members etc. A co-ordinated response to offer this help would involve a family supporter who would inform the appropriate agencies of the murder or manslaughter. Schools would be informed of the need to offer extra support to any child involved in the aftermath of this crime and how to offer it appropriately. Health services would be informed so that medical care could be offered in an appropriate and timely manner. Employers could be informed when a worker became a secondary victim and that employees' rights could be explained to both parties. There would be the offer of someone to visit the family and let them discuss how the package of support was working and what else they might need.

The cost of such a service would have to be met. Nobody seems keen to take on such a commitment. It is a shame they have not worked out how much the impact of such a crime costs society. Siblings often fall into offending, the mental health of many members of the family suffers and leaves them unable to cope with day to day life. People commit suicide, lose their jobs and suffer physically debilitating illnesses. Families break under the pressure and need to be re-housed.

There is a cost to society when a family becomes bereaved by murder. Society has to pay that cost. It would be a benefit to us all if that cost were reduced by early interventions that could help the family to survive the aftermath. It would be of immeasurable benefit to those of us who will become the bereaved families of murder victims.

CHAPTER 23

The Plot Thins

Wendy fights on, championing the rights of families all the way. Families have the right to know when the perpetrator is released from prison. On the day I wrote this, families had no right to know when the perpetrator is released from Broadmoor. Marc worries that he may be walking down the street with his children and see a figure walking towards him. He will look up, as the distance between them closes, and find himself staring into the eyes of Andrew Cole.

I'm sure that this will not always be the case. When it changes, Wendy will be one of the people to thank for that change.

•   •   •

When I started writing this book, Wendy was still looking for answers to questions that have haunted her for years. A window was broken at the front of the bungalow and one at the back. The noise of the first breaking glass would have alerted William and Fiona. They wouldn't have lain on the bed waiting for the intruder to enter. Cole drove to hospital with a clump of hair clenched tightly in his right hand and a rucksack on his back. She has a nightmare that replays a scene with two killers entering the bungalow. One breaks in at the front, while the other breaks in round the back. When the car pulled up outside of the hospital, one of them ran away.

I was writing *Chapter 7* of this book, 'More Questions than Answers', when we wrote a letter to the Chief Constable of Dyfed Powys Police and asked if Wendy could view the police evidence file.

Two officers arrived in early one afternoon in March 2006. Paz Edwards is a big man with a loud voice and a good heart. He sat on Wendy's red sofa next to Mark Roach, who I've mentioned earlier in the book (the PC who was called to Llandod Hospital on prisoner duties at 4.30 in the morning). They wanted to know who I was. We explained that I was just Wendy's friend and no, not a lawyer. We may have forgotten to mention this book …

We explained the issues. Paz was certain that there was only one perpetrator of the crime. He went through the evidence. He explained that the blood was tested and belonged to Cole, William or Fiona. A blood spatter expert had attended the scene and described what the patterns suggested to him. These patterns described a fight between William and Cole that started in the bedroom.

William was in bed when he suffered his first injuries. The bed was covered in his blood.

Cole did drive the car to Llandod hospital. We saw photographs of the inside of the car. The steering wheel was covered in blood. The gear stick (it was an automatic but there is a thing to change gear) was also covered in blood, as was the driver's seat. The passenger seat had only a couple of drops of blood on it. They could have been sprayed on when Cole moved his arm.

We asked about the injuries to Cole. Mark Roach had seen them and he described that Cole's finger was nearly sliced off. The surgeons did have a good deal of work to do on his hand. Wendy asked about Cole's attempt to take an overdose while he was in Morriston, but Mark Roach said he didn't stay and knew nothing about it. We do believe this officer slid a little lower down in his seat as he spoke, though and he did look as if a slight blush had flushed his cheeks.

We wanted to know about Dr Hilsden. Why did he treat Cole before attending the bungalow and then describe a fair-haired male with no visible injuries? An ambulance had been called. The two police officers left the hospital because they felt it was a priority to see if there was a chance of saving the victims. The ambulance had arrived about the same time they had, within a very short space of time. The medics had attended William and Fiona. They saw immediately that they were dead. At the time of the murders, medics were not allowed to declare life extinct. A doctor had to be called. Dr Hilsden arrived. The police did not want anybody else interfering with the crime scene. Dr Hilsden knew Fiona personally. They didn't make him go and look at the bodies. There was no need. Dr Hilsden ticked the box and left.

It was such a relief. It was so good to know that William and Fiona had received medical attention immediately. It was so good to know that nobody else was involved. It was so good to hear that the case had been thoroughly investigated.

Wendy concluded the interview with the words she says to any professional, involved in this case, that she meets. 'Andrew Cole told the judge that, if he is released, he will kill again.' Both officers confirmed that they remembered this. 'If he is released and kills again,' she warned, 'I will visit the family of the victim and tell them about that knowledge. I will tell them that I have reminded professionals about it many times over the years. I will tell them which professionals I have reminded of this fact.' She smiled as she spoke, but I'm sure they knew that she had just added their names to the list. If Cole is released and he does kill again, there is a list of people who will be called to account. Wendy will be the one reading the names from that list.

We were both smiling as we said goodbye to the officers. Wendy described how yet another a hollow feeling in her stomach had left her. She described how a feeling of peace had descended upon her. There was so much more that she now understood.

We sat down to another cup of tea. Wendy sipped at the steaming Earl Grey and then a silly grin spread over her face.

'Ah ha!' she announced. 'The plot thins!'

Indeed it did. The plot had thinned tremendously and there was not so much to haunt Wendy. It was a pity she had been forced to wait almost ten years before she got answers to questions that she had repeatedly asked. It is one of those changes that she would like to see, to make life easier for other families.

I have accompanied Wendy on the last five years of her journey. I will accompany her, as her friend, on the rest of her journey through life, I am sure. I am glad I received my instructions to befriend her. She adds as much to my life as I hope that I add to hers.

But why were we meant to meet?

I know why I met her now. So do you. You are holding it in your hand. I always wanted to write a book but I thought that I didn't have an interesting story to tell. Wendy never wanted to write a book but she had an important story to tell. Stories are powerful things. They demand to be told. They'll find their way out. They find people and bring people together and make decisions for you and about you, until you're ready to pour their words onto the page.